BHOGA KĀRIKĀ
OF SADYOJYOTI

BHOGA KĀRIKĀ

of Sadyojyoti

With the Commentary of Aghora Śiva

An Introduction with English Translation

W. A. BORODY

MOTILAL BANARSIDASS PUBLISHERS
PRIVATE LIMITED • DELHI

First Edition: Delhi, 2005

ISBN: 81-208-2935-2

MOTILAL BANARSIDASS
41 U.A. Bungalow Road, Jawahar Nagar, Delhi 110 007
8 Mahalaxmi Chamber, 22 Bhulabhai Desai Road, Mumbai 400 026
236, 9th Main III Block, Jayanagar, Bangalore 560 011
203 Royapettah High Road, Mylapore, Chennai 600 004
Sanas Plaza, 1302 Baji Rao Road, Pune 411 002
8 Camac Street, Kolkata 700 017
Ashok Rajpath, Patna 800 004
Chowk, Varanasi 221 001

Printed in India
BY JAINENDRA PRAKASH JAIN AT SHRI JAINENDRA PRESS,
A-45 NARAINA, PHASE-I, NEW DELHI 110 028
AND PUBLISHED BY NARENDRA PRAKASH JAIN FOR
MOTILAL BANARSIDASS PUBLISHERS PRIVATE LIMITED,
BUNGALOW ROAD, DELHI 110 007

Dedicated
to the Memory of
Krishna Sivaraman

इदं नम ऋषिभ्यः पूर्वजेभ्यः
पूर्वेभ्यः पथिकृद्भ्यः

— ऋग्वेद संहिता
(x.14.15)

CONTENTS

PREFACE

The *Bhoga Kārikā* by Sadyojyoti (eighth century A.D.) is a collection of one hundred forty-six *kārikā* verses that both outline the basic Śaivite epistemological and ontological doctrine as well as refute the leading darśanas of the period, e.g., Sāṁkhya, Nyāya, Cārvāka, etc. Sadyojyoti wrote the *Bhoga Kārikā* as a companion text to his *Mokṣa Kārikā*, which explicates and defends the Śaivite soteriological doctrine. In the second *kārikā* of the *Bhoga Kārikā*, Sadyojyoti claims that the two texts were written to clarify both *bhoga* and *mokṣa* from the point of view of Āgamic Śaivism, specifically the *Raurava Āgama*.

The commentary on the *Bhoga Kārikā* by Aghora Śiva (twelfth century A.D.), the only known commentary to have been discovered to date, is brief and clearly written. Aghora Śiva is both exegetical and polemical. His exegesis involves the traditional method of explaining the sense of each verse or collection of verses according to the meaning of the particular terms within each verse and the meaning or interpretation of the text as a whole; as well, specific references to other texts and views are cited, as a means of amplifying and bolstering the view of the *kārikā* text. The polemical side of Aghora Śiva's commentary, while it stays close to the argument of the *kārikā* text, does digress on matters that reveal much about Aghora Śiva's own doctrinal position.

The form of Śaivism expressed in the Āgamas represents a completely self-contained and self-explained "cosmos" wherein every aspect of the devotee's existence is understood according to the Śaivite teaching. "Āgamic" Śaivism rests on doctrinal principles and behavioral criteria that are no less exacting than those established in the Vedic *śruti* and *smṛti* literature dealing with dharma and mokṣa.

While Āgamic Śaivism accepts as fundamental a basic devotion (*bhakti*) towards Śiva (and the pantheon of Śaivite demigods), a greater degree of importance is placed on the inherent efficaciousness of the consecratory and sacramental rites (*dīkṣā*)governing the devotee's life and soteriological development. Coupled with this notion of the importance of the purificatory rites the Śaivite Āgamas also place a corresponding degree of emphasis on the soteriological importance of a "discerning insight" in the *jñāna-pada* sections. It is exactly this "discerning insight" of the Āgamas that Sadyojyoti treats in the *Bhoga Kārikā,* essentially in the context of epistemology and ontology.

The *Bhoga Kārikā* is of seminal importance for an understanding of the history of Śaivite philosophical and theological thought. Indeed, in terms of the history of Indian philosophy, the conciseness, originality and logical forcefulness of the *Bhoga Kārikā* rivals the *Sāṁkhya Kārikā*; in terms of expository clarity, the Commentary by Aghora Śiva stands on an equal footing with Vācaspati Miśra's *Tattva Kaumudi.*

I began the translation of the *Bhoga Kārikā* and Aghora Śiva's commentary during a one-year fellowship residency in Chennai, which was funded by the Shastri Indo-Canadian Institute. I thank the Institute for having provided me with the opportunity to carry out research in India. I would also like to thank the late Dr. S.S. Janaki, director of the Kuppuswami Sastri Research Institute, who took time off from her busy schedule to read the Sanskrit text of the *Bhogakārikāvṛtti* with me and to introduce me to the world of the traditional Indian Scholar. The excellent facilities at the Kuppuswami Sastri Research Institute and the stimulation derived from the scholars and assistants associated with the centre helped facilitate the progress of this work. Also, I would like to thank the Nipissing University Research Council for generously providing me with a publication grant. For both the genesis and completion of this work in its initial stage as a section of my doctoral thesis, I express my gratitude, the gratitude of a *śiṣya,* to Drs. K. Sivaraman, J. G. Ararpura, W. Whillier and P. Granoff.

Finally, for the support only those close to one can give, and gave unreservedly during the preparation of this work, I would like to thank Candy, Calin, Gabriel, Ron, Judy, Patrick, and my mother and father.

—W.A. Borody

ABBREVIATIONS

AP	:	*Aṣṭa Prakaraṇa*
BK	:	*Bhoga Kārikā*
BKV	:	*Bhoga Kārikā Vṛtti*
MĀ	:	*Mṛgendra Āgama*
MĀD	:	*Mṛgendra Āgama Dīpikā*
MĀV	:	*Mṛgendra Āgama Vṛtti*
MPĀ	:	*Mataṅga Parameśvara Āgama*
MPAV	:	*Mataṅga Parameśvarāgama Vṛtti*
RĀ	:	*Raurava Āgama*
ŚPB	:	*Śaiva Paribhāṣā*
ŚTS	:	*Śata Ratna Saṁgraha*
ŚRU	:	*Śata Ratna Ullekha*
TP	:	*Tattva Prakāśa*
TS(V)	:	*Tattva Saṁgraha (Vṛtti)*
TTNV	:	*Tattva Traya Nirṇaya Vṛtti*

INTRODUCTION

1. Author

According to all available evidence, Sadyojyoti, the author of the *Bhoga Kārikā,* flourished during the eighth century A.D. This date is arrived at through the more established dating of other Śaivite authors and texts. The *terminus ad quem* for Sadyojyoti's writings is placed prior to the beginning of the ninth century, which is the time one of his commentators, Rāmakaṇṭha II, has been established to have flourished.[1] There are no means to establish securely the earliest period of Sadyojyoti's writings except through the very general dating of the earliest dated Śaiva *Āgamas,* as Sadyojyoti is considered to have commented on at least two of these *Āgamas.* Scholars are divided, however, as to the precise century the *Āgamas* were first composed; after a consideration of the available historical and textual evidence concerning this period, J. Gonda has suggested the seventh century A.D. as the earliest possible dating.[2] Thus, as a compromise between the earliest and latest datings of works having direct relevance to his works, Sadyojyoti is considered to have flourished approximately in the eighth century.[3]

Sadyojyoti's works fall into two genres: either commentaries on *Āgamas* or manuals (*prakaraṇa*) summarizing the Śaiva "*darśana*", i.e., view of the world – "philosophy" in the classical sense.[4] Sadyojyoti is said to have written a commentary on the *Raurava Āgama*; he himself claims to have written a commentary on the *Svāyambhuva Āgama.*[5] Although more will be said of Sadyojyoti's apparent commentary on the *Raurava Āgama* in the sequel, it is sufficient at this point to mention that the commentary has not been recovered. His commentary on the *Svāyambhuva Āgama*, which he mentions in one of his own manuals, exists in an incomplete form[6]. Although the exact number of philosophical manuals that Sadyojyoti composed has not been established, five have survived. Originally, these manuals may have been written for inclusion in an *Āgama* as specific treatments of certain topics. All the manuals are written in very concise and complex argumentative verses (*kārikā*); without the commentaries that accompany each of the manuals, it is doubtful whether modern scholars or traditionally trained Śaiva pundits could discern the intent of the verses, although this is not to suggest that the early commentators are always correct in their interpretations of the original verses. According to Sadyojyoti in the opening line of the *Bhoga Kārikā*, the *Mokṣa Kārikā* and *Bhoga Kārikā* actually form one complete text, although the complete text was early on chosen by the commentators as two separate texts.

Aghora Śiva (twelfth century) has commented on the *Bhoga Kārikā* while Rāmakaṇṭha II (ninth century) has commented on the *Mokṣa Kārikā*. While the *Bhoga Kārikā* opens with the appropriate statement of obeisance (*maṅgala*), the *Mokṣa Kārikā* ends with a traditional colophon stating some detail about the author. Aghora Śiva has also commented on the *Tattva Saṁgraha*[7] and the *Tattva Traya Nirṇaya*; the former work summarily describes the entire Śaivite cosmology while the latter specifically discusses the relationship between the three basic Śaivite categories of God, bondage and the soul. The *Paramokṣa Nirāsa Kārikā* deals with the refutation of other doctrines of release and has been commented on by Rāmakaṇṭha II.

In the works that still survive, neither Sadyojyoti nor his commentators provide much in the way of biographical detail. In the *Tattva Saṁgraha* the author refers to himself as "Sadyojyoti, the author of the Good Commentary [or "the good commentator"] (*suvṛttikṛt*)."[8] Aghora Śiva takes this to mean that Sadyojyoti is the author of the *sadvṛtti*, a commentary on the *Raurava Āgama*.[9] In his own conclusion to the *Tattva Saṁgraha* Aghora Śiva refers to Sadyojyoti as Kheṭakanandana; other authors also refer to him by this name.[10] In the closing verses of the *Tattva Traya Nirṇaya* Sadyojyoti refers to himself as the author of the commentary on the *Svāyambhuva Āgama*.[11] In the closing verse of the *Mokṣa Kārikā* the author refers to himself as "Sadyojyoti" and to his teacher as "Ugrajyoti"; he further says that his teaching ultimately derives from Śiva who revealed it to the sage Ruru who in turn passed it on to Ātreya, from whom Sadyojyoti received it.[12] Rāmakaṇṭha II pays particular respect to Sadyojyoti as one of the founders of the Śaiva-darśana:[13] "Among the masters one should pay particular respect to Sadyojyoti and Bṛhaspati,[14] who have illuminated the path of the Śaiva position through their accomplished virtues."

After Aghora Śiva (twelfth century), Sadyojyoti's works no longer gained the attention of serious commentators, although even during the fourteenth century Sadyojyoti is still recognized as an authoritative representative of the Śaiva doctrine, as he is quoted, for example, in both the *Śata Ratna Ullekha*[15] and in Mādhava *Sarva Darśana Saṁgraha*.[16] In the later development of the Śaivite tradition, Sadyojyoti is considered to be one of the eighteen renowned authors of manuals.[17]

One can gather from such textual references that Sadyojyoti considered himself and was considered by others to be an authoritative and exalted spokesperson of the Śaiva tradition. As well, it can be concluded that he represented the tradition of the *Raurava Āgama* and *Svāyambhuva Āgama*. He may also have written his philosophical manuals in order to clarify the Śaivite position on points of doctrine over which the various Āgamas differed.

Whether he was from northern or southern India remains an unanswered question, since both Aghora Śiva, a Tamil, and Rāmakaṇṭha II, a Kashmiri, wrote commentaries on

Sadyojyoti's works; however, since Rāmakaṇṭha II predates Aghora Śiva by two centuries, one is led to suspect that Sadyojyoti is originally from the north and that his works travelled to the south.[18]

2. *Bhoga Kārikā* and the *Raurava Āgama*

The connection between the *Bhoga Kārikā* and the *Raurava Āgama* is of direct concern to the work at hand as is the relation between Sadyojyoti's *Bhoga Kārikā* and the *Raurava Āgama,* as the *Bhoga Kārikā* claims to describe *bhoga* in terms of the tradition established by Ruru, the supposed sage of the *Raurava Āgama.*

In the second verse of the *Bhoga Kārikā* Sadyojyoti says that he is going to describe mundane experience and release, i.e., *bhoga* and *mokṣa,* "in accordance with the teaching of Ruru (*rurusiddhāntasaṁsiddhau bhogamokṣau sasādhanau vacmi*)."[19] Aghora Śiva explains that this means "in accordance with the *Raurava Āgama* (*śrīmadrauravatantra-upalakṣitasiddhāntaśāstre*)."[20] As will be pointed out in the sequel, there are specific points of doctrinal agreement between Sadyojyoti and the philosophical position of the *Raurava Āgama* to warrant Aghora Śiva's identification of Ruru's teaching with the *Raurava Āgama.* However, there is less reason to accept, as is generally accepted,[21] Aghora Śiva's and Rāmakaṇṭha II's assertion that Sadyojyoti is in fact the author of a *Raurava Vṛtti,* which Aghora Śiva specifically refers to as the *Sadvṛtti.* There are two problems with this identification. First, although Sadyojyoti refers to himself as the author of the good commentary (*suvṛttikṛt*) in the *Tattva Saṁgraha,*[22] he does not mention the text to which he refers; this reference to a "*Suvṛttikṛt*" could indeed refer to Sadyojyoti's commentary on the *Svāyambhuva Āgama* which he refers to in the closing verse of the *Tattva Traya Nirṇaya,* describing himself as the commentator (*vṛttikṛt*) of the *Svāyambhuva Āgama.*[23] Secondly, there is a problem with Aghora Śiva's description of the title of Sadyojyoti's *Raurava Vṛtti* as the

Sadvṛtti since Śrīkaṇṭha in the closing verses of his *Ratna Traya* claims that his mentor, Rāmakaṇṭha I, wrote a "*Sadvṛtti*", which Śrīkaṇṭha has modeled his own *Ratna Traya* after.[24] In his commentary on the *Ratna Traya* Aghora Śiva peculiarly says nothing about the reference to the *Sadvṛtti*.[25] Although Rāmakaṇṭha II mentions a *Raurava Vṛtti* in his commentary on the *Mataṅga Pārameśvara Āgama,* he does not actually quote from it; as well, it is difficult to discern whether or not he is referring to his own commentary on a certain *Raurava Vṛtti* called the *Raurava Vṛtti Viveka* or to the position of the *Raurava Vṛtti* itself.[26] This confusion over the authorship of the commentary on the *Raurava Āgama* is further compounded by the fact that the commentary no longer exists, or at least has not been discovered. Nor is the "*Raurava Vṛtti*" quoted by the commentors most familiar with Sadyojyoti's works, i.e., Aghora Śiva and Rāmakaṇṭha II; and an actual citation from a certain *Raurava Āgama Vṛtti* in the commentary on the *Mataṅga Pārameśvara Āgama* is actually a verse from Sadyojyoti's *Paramokṣa Nirāsa Kārikā*.[27] If there had been such a *Vṛtti* on the *Raurava Āgama* and indeed if it had been written by Sadyojyoti, the likelihood exists that it no longer existed by the time Rāmakaṇṭha II and Aghora Śiva came to write their commentaries on Sadyojyoti's manuals.

3. The Doctrinal Relation between the *Bhoga Kārikā* and the *Raurava Āgama*

Ideally, each *Āgama* contains four sections that treat philosophy (*jñāna-pāda*), yogic discipline (*yoga-pāda*), ritual (*kriyā-pāda*) and conduct (*caryā-pāda*). To date, only the sections dealing with philosophy and ritual have been recovered from the *Raurava Āgama*. The philosophical section of the *Raurava Āgama,* which has been edited by N.R. Bhatt of the French Institute of Indology, is most likely an incomplete, abridged version of a larger text; most of the manuscripts of the *Raurava Āgama* actually refer to it as the *Raurava Sūtra Saṁgraha* in the colophon of each sub-section *(paṭala)*.[28] Bhatt suggests that the *Raurava Sūtra Saṁgraha* has been taken for the *Raurava Āgama* itself since the twelfth century, as is evident from the fact that the various commentators of the philosophical manuals refer to it as if it were the *Āgama;* if the text of the *Raurava* that we possess is actually the *Āgama,* it may be referred to as a "summary" since, like other *Āgamas,* it claims to be a summary of a much larger treatise.[29]

In his discussion of the importance of the *Raurava Āgama* in light of Āgamic literature, Bhatt distinguishes three things which make its section on philosophy of interest in the light of other *Āgamas;* first, the exposition of yoga lists just six stages of yoga instead of the traditional eight as passed down by Patañjali;[30] secondly, the *tattvas* are listed as thirty whereas in most of the *Āgamas* and manuals they are listed as thirty-six – Śakti, Sadāśiva, Īśvara, Śuddhavidyā, Kāla and Niyati are omitted in the *Raurava;*[31] thirdly, in the manuscripts of the *Raurava Āgama* which have been discovered so far, there is no evidence that the twelve verses which form the *Śiva-Jñāna Bodha,* the locus classicus of the Tamil "Meykandar School", come from the *Raurava Āgama,* a claim upheld by commentators on the *Śivajñāna Bodha,* although this is not to say that in the future a more complete text of the philosophical section will be found which will contain the twelve verses.[32]

Of more specific concern to the connection between the *Bhoga Kārikā* and the *Raurava Āgama* one can point to Sadyojyoti's claim in the first verse that he is going to explain *bhoga* according to the teaching of Ruru. In the *Raurava Āgama,* Ruru is said to be the only one who can cause the understanding of Śiva (*śivajñānaikāraṇa*).[33] The object of Ruru's discourse is the instruction of other sages in the understanding of Śaivite doctrine. Like Sadyojyoti in the *Bhoga Kārikā,* Ruru speaks in the first person. He says that other sages have come to him, i.e., Bhārgava, Aṅgiras, Ātreya and Marīci, in great obeisance to ask him to reveal the nature of the Śaivite doctrine and the enumeration of the *tattvas.*[34]

Doctrinal similarity between the *Bhoga Kārikā* and the *Raurava Āgama* can also be found in the basic metaphysical view shared by both works, viz., a pantheistic dualism wherein the Supreme Being Śiva is both immanent in the world and at the same time transcendent to it, a condition that applies to the soul as well. Although Śiva is, on the one hand, "beyond" the world and any connections to it, he is, through the agency of Sadāśiva, engaged and immanent "in the world". Objectively, Sadāśiva, is described as the creator of the world and time–indeed, of "everything" (*sarvakṛt*), including the gods Brahmā etc.; subjectively, he is described as residing in the self of all things (*sarvabhūtātmabhūtastha*). Sadāśiva is "the soul of the world (*parātma*)."[35]

Throughout the *Vidyāpāda* of the *Raurava Āgama* solar imagery is employed to describe the relation between the world and Śiva. Śiva is described as a source of light while the world is described as the light itself (qua śakti).[36] *Śivajñāna* is said to cause the supreme "illumination" for those who are "blinded" by the darkness of the bonds. The primordial impurity (*mala* or *añjāna*) is the primordial darkness. Although Śiva is devoid of this impurity he engages in it in order to "purify" it and bring about the "illumination" of the estranged souls. The dualism between Śiva and the world begins with the separation of Śiva from a host of lower gods who carry out the various worldly superintending activities;[37] these gods are described as Śiva's own "rays of illumination (*svakiraṇa*)." The imagery of light and darkness is employed in the *Raurava Āgama* both cosmologically and soteriologically in order to explain the benefits conferred upon the initiate through Śiva's "śakti".

Concerning the specific enumeration of the *tattvas*, Sadyojyoti is in close agreement with the *Raurava Āgama* in leaving out "time" (*kāla*) and "limitation" (*niyati*) from the account of the *tattvas* from *kalā* to the earth. In the *Raurava Āgama* the cosmic function of "time" is ascribed to Śiva in his form as Sadāśiva, who is "the instigator of all time" (*sarvakālapravartaka*) and "the lord of time" (*kālādhipa*).[38]

A similar approach to "time" as a pre-tattvic factor of creation is also found in the *Bhoga Kārikā*. Although "limitation", the factor that limits each soul to specific life experiences and temporal events, is not mentioned in the *Raurava Āgama,* the *Bhoga Kārikā* discusses it in non-tattvic terms as the working out of each soul's *karma,* which is ultimately under the guidance of Śiva. As well, neither the *Raurava Āgama* nor the *Bhoga Kārikā* treat the soul as a *tattva,* i.e., the *puruṣattva,* as do other forms of Āgamic Śaivism. For the above discussed reasons, there appears to be sufficient reason to hold that the teaching of Ruru referred to in the *Bhoga Kārikā* actually refers to the teaching established in the *Raurava Āgama,* as Aghora Śiva asserts.

4. Aghora Śiva, the Commentator of the *Bhoga Kārikā*

Aghora Śiva, who flourished during the twelfth century, was not only an accomplished poet, dramatist and commentator, but also a religious leader of renown, with a very large number of followers.[39] He tells us that he is from the Cola country, i.e., Tamilnadu; although he is a southerner, in one of his works he claims to represent the teachings of Rāmakaṇṭha II, a Kāshmirī. As a testament to Aghora Śiva's importance and authority in the Śaiva tradition, his works on ritual are said to be conscientiously followed by all the Śaiva priests in the South to this day.[40]

Since Aghora Śiva chose to comment on three of Sadyojyoti's works, one must conclude that he was well-acquainted with Sadyojyoti's thought. From Aghora Śiva's commentary on the *Mṛgendra Āgama Vṛtti* by Rāmakaṇṭha II it is evident that Aghora Śiva was very well-acquainted with the Śaivite philosophical doctrine and the positions of many other Āgamas. Although Sadyojyoti claims to represent one Āgamic tradition in the *Bhoga Kārikā,* namely the *Raurava Āgama,* Aghora Śiva appeals to many *Āgamas* to justify his views, namely *Kiraṇa, Raurava, Svāyambhuva, Mataṅga, Mṛgendra,* etc. As a commentator, Aghora Śiva is clear and consistent. His commentarial aim is expository, usually carried out through word by word or phrase by phrase analysis. His own doctrinal concerns are always clear. Three such concerns are often expressed in his commentary on the *Bhoga Kārikā: dīkṣā* and not *jñāna* is the major prerequisite for *mokṣa;* Śiva has no direct material contact with anything worldly, as Śiva is solely the instrumental cause and not the material cause of the world; and lastly, there are no doctrinal contradictions among the various Āgamic teachings.

The particular style of Aghora Śiva's commentarial writings on Sadyojyoti's manuals is most clear when a comparison is drawn between Aghora Śiva's commentary on Bhoja Deva's *Tattva Prakāśa* (eleventh century A.D.)and the commentary on the same text by Śrī Kumāra, a clear exponent of Śaiva monism. While Śrī Kumāra quotes many Vedic texts (e.g., the *Upaniṣads* and *Brāhmaṇas, Purāṇas* and *Āgamas*), Aghora Śiva ignores the Vedic material and *Purāṇas* and solely relies on the *Āgamas.* Again, while Śrī Kumāra stresses logical and definitional clarity in his interpretation of the verses, Aghora Śiva stresses the scriptural authority of the Śaivite Āgamas to explain and justify the ideas in the verses.

5. The Manner in which "Mundane-Experience", i.e., "*Bhoga*", is Introduced in the *Bhoga Kārikā*

The *Bhoga Kārikā* consists of one hundred and forty-six verses. In the first four verses Sadyojyoti both introduces and summarizes his treatment of the concept of "*bhoga*", i.e., "mundane-experience". He begins with a traditional obeisance (*maṅgalācaraṇa*) to Śiva and an outline of the work (*anubandha*).[41] The outline is fourfold, describing the subject matter (*viṣaya*), and the purpose of the work (*prayojana*), the method of treatment (*saṁgati*) and finally, the person for whom the work is written (*adhikārin*). In due order, the subject matter is said to be the dual topics of mundane-experience and release; the purpose concerns the facilitation of "the discernment" of these two topics; the method of treatment is said to proceed according to "tradition, logic,[42] and brevity"[43]; and the person for whom the work is composed is described as "the *sādhaka*",[44] i.e., of one engaged in the quest for *Śiva-jñāna.*

At the outset, Śiva is described as the one who "provides" or "gives" both mundane-experience and release. By stating this at the outset of the *Bhoga Kārikā,* Sadyojyoti is expressing a basic Śaivite theological concern that the soul is not the sole "cause" or "means" (*nimitta*) of its soteriological station in mundane existence. Ultimately, the Śaivite argues, the supreme being, Śiva, is the instrumental cause of all of the soul's experiences.

In a cosmological sense, mundane-experience is said to arise when those souls who have the "triple bonds" come in contact with *kalā,* the manifesting agency of mundane-experience qua individual consciousness.[45] The "triple bonds" include *mala,* the original obscurational factor inhibiting the soul's innate consciousness and omnipotence, *karma,* the repository and instrumental agency of the particular defilements of each individual soul, and *māyā,* the more specific obscurational cause of the soul's absorption in the condition of mundane-experience. This bound condition describes the more cosmic side of mundane-experience since *kalā* actually originates from *māyā* or can be said to be one of the specific manifestations of *māyā*–thus making the three "bonds" characterize the mundane condition of the soul.

Ultimately, according to the Śaivites, there are only three basic "categories" (*padārtha*) of reality: God, souls and bonds.[46] "Bond" in this sense is another term to designate that which experientially limits the full capacity of the soul's innate powers of consciousness and agency. In Sadyojyoti's works one discovers a tendency to see *mala* itself as representative of the category of bond (*pāśa*), i.e., as the obscurational and defiling power (*rodhaśakti*) responsible for the soul's predicament in the condition of *bhoga.* Thus, all bonds are referred to as material (*jaḍa*) and unconscious (*acetana*) and are set in cosmic opposition to the soul which is of a non-material and conscious nature. *Bhoga* simply represents the predicament of the soul when it is involved in this cosmic opposition.

Sadyojyoti adds a further, more specific, description of *bhoga* which brings out the psychological sense of the notion. The term "*bhoga*" literally means "enjoyment" and in this psychological account of *bhoga* the idea of "enjoyment" plays an important role. Sadyojyoti expresses the classical yogic idea that *bhoga* is the "*buddhi-vṛtti anurañjana*"—the (impassioned) attachment to the modifications of the mind.[47] The conception of the "modifications of the mind" (*buddhi-vṛtti*) is based on the distinction between the soul qua source of consciousness and the mind as constitutive of the experiential "object" of the soul's consciousness. The mind is simply that in which and through which empirically circumscribed consciousness comes to be; the mind is that in which and through which the bonds of the triadically bound soul come to form "empirical" or "mundane" forms of consciousness for individual souls. The modifications of the mind act as the final instantiation of the "limited" condition of the soul in its empirical predicament. The limitation is a result of the soul's empathetic identification with the modifications of the mind; due to the establishment of this empathetic identification circumscribed by the condition of *bhoga*, the mind appears as anything but "unconscious" and "material".

The term Sadyojyoti uses for this condition of the soul's empathetic identification with the "*buddhi-vṛtti*" is "*anurañjana*", which literally means to be coloured by something, "enreddened" in the sense of "passionately attached to" as well as "endarkened" in the sense of "obscured". "*Anurañjana*" is a condition not only of "impassionment" but "delusion", both of which are a result of the modifications of the mind.

Throughout the *Bhoga Kārikā*, Sadyojyoti plays on the two-fold sense of "*bhoga*" as both "experience" and "enjoyment". As the empathetic identification with the *buddhi-vṛtti*, "*bhoga*" is something the soul "wants" and "enjoys" in spite of the fact that *bhoga* is essentially an "impure" condition of "self-estrangement". It is precisely this element of pleasure constitutive of bhogic experience that the notion of *anurañjana* addresses. *Bhoga* is not only a certain kind of "experience" but at the same time the desire for this experience.

If it were not for the grace of Śiva the soul would be eternally caught in the enjoyment of mundane-experience through continual rebirths. Out of "graciousness", Śiva grants the possibility of the separation from *bhoga* for the snapping asunder of the obfuscating and empathetic identification with the *buddhi-vṛtti*. *Bhoga* is a privation of the soul's innate capacities of consciousness and agency; *mokṣa* is the overcoming of this privation. However, although *bhoga* is the only means souls have open to them to bring about *mokṣa, mokṣa* cannot solely be considered a more developed condition of *bhoga,* a more "cultivated" or "refined" form of bhoga. Soteriologically, *bhoga* is only a "means" to *mokṣa.*

Endnotes

1. Bhatt establishes the date of Rāmakaṇṭha II in an indirect manner that is ultimately based on the dating of Abhinavagupta. In his *MĀV* Nārāyaṇakaṇṭha cites a verse from Utpaladeva (*Īśvarasiddhi,* v. 55, *KSTS,* Vol. 24, 1921, p. 30). Utpaladeva is known to be the peer of Lakṣmaṇagupta, the mentor of Abhinavagupta, who states in his *Tantrāloka,* 12.25: "Utpaladeva is the master of my master". Utpaladeva is therefore established to have flourished around the second half of the ninth c. As a result, it can be inferred that Nārāyaṇakaṇṭha and Rāmakaṇṭha II are prior to the beginning of the ninth century; cf. *Matāṅgapārameśvara Āgama* (*Vidyāpāda*), critically edited by N.R. Bhatt, *Publications de L'Institut Français d'Indologie,* No. 56 (Pondicherry: Institut Français d'Indologie, No. 56 (Pondicherry:

Institut Français d'Indologie, 1997), pp. vii-viii. Since Rāmakaṇṭha II commented on two of sadyojyoti's works and since Rāmakaṇṭha II considers Sadyojyoti to be one of "the venerable ancient masters" indicating that some time must have passed between Sadyojyoti and Rāmakaṇṭha II – the eighth century. This does not, however, rule out the possibility that Sadyojyoti's date might be much earlier.

2. A precise date for the oldest *Āgamas* cannot be established although various dates have been suggested. For example, Dasgupta suggests that the earliest Āgamas began to be composed in the second or third centuries; see Surendranath Dasgupta, *A History of Indian Philosophy* (Varanasi: Motilal Banarsidass, 1975), II, 40. Although Jan Gonda accepts that the earliest *Āgamas* may have been composed between the fifth and the ninth centuries he concludes his discussion of the various datings put forth by other authors by restricting the earliest dating to the seventh or eighth century; cf. Jan Gonda, "Medieval Religious Literature in Sanskrit," Vol. II, Fasçicle I, *A History of Indian Literature,* ed. Jan Gonda (Wiesbaden; Otto Harrassowitz, 1977), pp. 163-165. In passing it may be noted that the Śaivite *Śvetāśvatara Upaniṣad* is generally held to have been composed around the fifth or fourth century B.C.; see Jan Gonda, *Viṣṇuism and Śaivism: A Comparison* (New Delhi: Munshiram Manoharlal, 1976), p. 18.

3. Pandey suggests the ninth century, although he does not provide the specific reasons for this dating; however, he probably adopted it as a compromise between Rāmkaṇṭha II's dating and an early dating of the Āgamas; see K.C. Pandey, "*Bhāskarī,*" Vol. III, The Princess of Wales Saraswati Bhavana Texts, ed. by T.P. Upadhyana, No. 84 (Lucknow: Superintendent, Printing and Stationary, U.P., 1954), p. xv.

4. A style of work which would not fit into these genres would be the *Mantravārttika* attributed to Sadyojyoti by Rāmakaṇṭha II in his commentary on the *MK*, p.4. The *Mantravārttika* has not been recovered.

5. In the closing verse of the *Tattva Traya Nirṇaya* (v. 32, p. 21) Sadyojyoti refers to himself as the commentator (*vṛttikṛt*) of the *Svāyambhuva Āgama* and claims that the *Tattva Traya Nirṇaya* is written according to the teaching of the *Svāyambhuva Āgama.*

6. The *Svāyambhuva Āgama* — entitled the *Syāyambhuva-sūtrasaṁgrahavṛttiḥ* — whose incomplete commentary is attributed to Sadyojyoti contains the first four sections of *Jñānapāda* which deal with *Pati, Paśu, Śakti* and *Adhva*. Various other Śaivite authors refer to this commentary by Sadyojyoti as *svāyambhuvasūtraṭīkā, svāyambhuvavṛtti, svāyambhuvasūtrasaṅgraha-vṛtti* and *svāyambhuvaśāstraṭīkā;* see Bhatt *Mataṅgapārameśvara Āgama*, pp. xvi-xvii. It is also referred to as the *sadyojyotiṣṭīkā*; cf. Pandit Panchan Sastri. "*Śataratna saṁgraha with Śataratnollekha,*" intro. by Shrimat Svami Bhairabanada, Tantrik Texts, ed. Arthur Avalon, vol. xxii (Calcutta: Agamanusandhan Samiti, 1944), p. 83. In terms of *Āgamic* chronology, the *Svāyambhuva Āgama* is prior to the *Raurava Āgama* as Ruru refers to the former work in 3.14 of the *Raurava Āgama*. Pierre-Sylvain Filliozat has edited and translated (into English) the *Svāyambhuva-sūtrasaṅgraha-vṛtti.*
7. In his commentary on the *TS,* Aghora Śiva mentions a "long commentary" (*bṛhaṭṭīkā*) called the *śaranniśā* by Nārāyaṇakaṇṭha of which his own, which he describes as "a short commentary" (*laghuṭīkā*), is modeled after.
8. v. 57; *TS,* p. 52.
9. *TS,* p. 52: "*suvṛttiḥ sadvṛttiriti rauravavṛtternāma tatkartredaṁ nirmitamityarthaḥ.*"
10. For example, cf. also *MĀV,* p. 153. Sadyojyoti is also referred to as Kheṭakabāla in *MPV,* p. 72. He is referred to as Kheṭapāla in Jayaratha's commentary on the *Tantrāloka.*
11. *Tattva Traya Nirṇaya,* v. 32, p. 21
12. *Mokṣa Kārikā* v. 155 "*śivātparaṁparāyātau bhogamokṣau sasādhanau/ ātreyāya munīndreṇa ruruṇā saṁprakāśitau.*" In the *Śivamahāpurāṇa* the twenty-eight original Yogācāryas are enumerated. Each of the twenty-eight had four disciples of which a certain "Ruru" is said to be a prominent one; cf. *Vāyavīya Saṃhitā,* 2, 9. The *Raurava Āgama* is said to be communicated by the sage Ruru to "Marīci" who is an ancient sage and demiurge; the mental son of Brahmā.
13. "*Yābhyāṁ prakāśitaṁ vartma siddhānte siddhabhāvataḥ gurūṇāmapi tau vandyau sadyojyotibṛhaspatī.*" This *maṅgalaśloka* is found in both the *MKV,* p. 2 and the *MPV,* p. 1.
14. The *Tantrāloka* (1.104A) states: "in the *Śivatanuśāstra* the Lord is revealed by the masters". Jayaratha's comments that "masters" refers to Bṛhaspati; the plural is honourific.

15. The *Mokṣa Kārikā* is quoted in the commentary on v. 27; the *Tattva Saṁgraha* is quoted in the commentary on vv. 40, 41, and 76.
16. Mādhava quotes *TS* 24B-25A and Aghora Śiva's commentary thereon.
17. For the list of the eighteen renowned authors of manuals, i.e., Ugrajyoti, Sadyojyoti, Rāmakaṇṭha, Somaśambhu, Aghora Śambhu, etc.; see H. Brunner-Lachaux, *Somaśambhu-Paddhati,* Publications de l'Institut Français d'Indologie, 2 Vol., No. 25 (Pondicherry: Institut Français d'Indologie, 1963, 1968), I, xxii. Śrī Umāpati quotes from the *Mokṣa Kārikā, Tattva Traya Nirṇaya* and *Tattva Saṁgraha:* see the *Śataratnollekha* commentary on verses 21, 27, 40, 41 and 76.
18. Rāmakaṇṭha II claims that he is from Kashmir in the last verse of his *Nāda Kārikā* and Aghora Śiva claims that he is from the region of the Cola both in the *TTNV* and *Kriyākramadyotikā.* Since Rāmakaṇṭha II is earlier than Aghora Śiva it is more plausible that Sadyojyoti is also from Kashmir and that the works of Sadyojyoti and Rāmkaṇṭha II were brought to the south. Aghora Śiva claims to remain faithful to the "teaching" of Rāmakaṇṭha II (*MĀD,* p. 1); see also Bhatt, *MP,* p. ix x.
19. *BK,* v. 2A
20. *BKV* on v. 2A.
21. See, for example, Pandey, *Bhāskarī* p. xvi and Bhatt, *Mataṅgapārameśvara Āgama,* p. xvi.
22. TS, v. 57: "*ityavadatattvāni tu sadyojyotiḥ suvṛttikṛt.*"
23. *Tattva Traya Nirṇaya,* v. 32.
24. *Ratna Traya,* v. 319; "*śrīrāmakaṇṭhasadvṛttiṁ mayaivamanukurvata.*" This problem is even further complicated by the reference to a *sadvṛttiḥ* by a certain *Śrīrāma;* for a discussion of this problem see Bhatt, *MPĀ,* p. xiv.
25. Aghora Śiva adds almost no commentary to the last six verses.
26. see *MPĀV* (3, 19), p. 68. The text reads: "*darśitamasmābhiḥ ...rauravavṛttiviveke iti.*" Bhatt takes this to refer to the *Rauravavṛttiviveka* by Rāmakaṇṭha II.
27. In the *MPĀV* the quotation from the so-called "*Rauravāgamavṛttiḥ*" actually refers to v. 52 of the *Paramokṣa Nirāsa Kārikā;* in the *MPĀV* Rāmakaṇṭha II may simply be referring to his commentary on either this work or the *Mokṣa Kārikā;* see *MPĀV,* p. 609.

28. With respect to the title of the *Raurava Āgama* as the *Raurava-"sūtra-" Saṁgraha, Āgamic* writers loosely refer to the verses as sūtras rather than ślokas; cf. *MA,* I, 27.
29. Compared to the *Jñānapādas* of other *Āgamas,* such as the *Mataṅga* and *Mṛgendra,* the *Jñānapāda* of the *Raurava Āgama* is very paltry. In the *Raurava Āgama* itself Ruru says that the *Āgama* was first revealed in different forms by the five faces of SadāŚiva and was later reconstituted by Anantapārameśvara to form one crore of ślokas, which Ruru further condensed to 1200. The present edition of the *Vidyāpāda* contains 399 Ślokas. If all the ślokas from the *Kriyāpāda* are taken into account the present *Raurava Āgama* would contain well over 1,200 ślokas. For a summary of the ten sections of the *Jñānapāda* of *Raurava Āgama.* See Gonda, *Medieval Religious Literature in Sanskrit,* p. 169-170.
30. See *RĀ,* 7.5 For a discussion of the Śaivite conception of "yoga" cf. Dasgupta, op. cit. p. 204. Bhatt mentions the listing of the Āṅgas in other *Āgamas*: *Mataṅgapāramaśvara* (*Yogapāda, paṭala* 1) lists the same six; *MĀ* (*yoga-pāda, paṭala* 3) lists the same six but adds *Japa*; *Kiraṇāgama* (*yogapāda, paṭala* 1) lists six but replaces the *tarka* of *RĀ* with *āsana*; and the *Suprabhedāgama* (*yogapāda, paṭala* 3) lists the eight given in the *Yogasūtras.*
31. Actually, an exact numerical enumeration of the tattvas does not appear to be a concern of the *RA*; for instance, in some sections "manas" is included among an enumeration of the tattvas while elsewhere it is excluded (cf. 1.13 and 4.49). Although throughout the *RĀ* the five Śivatattvas (Śiva, Śakti, Sadāśiva, Īśvara, and Śuddhavidyā) are discussed in the exposition of the *Śaivadarśana* in 10, 98-101 they are not included in a numerical exposition of the tattvas.
32. Certain Tamil commentators on the *Śivajñānabodha* claim that the *Śivajñānabodha* is a portion of the twelfth *adhyāya* of the seventy-third *paṭala* of the *RĀ* designated as the "*pāśavimocanapaṭala*"; as well, in the Kannada speaking area of the south there is a legend that a teacher called "*Śivajñānabodha*" wrote the twelve verses as a condensed version "of the essence" of the RĀ. For a discussion of the Meykaṇḍar literature, see K. Sivaraman, *Śaivism in Philosophical Perspective* (Varaṇasi: Motilal Banarsidass, 1973), pp. 30-39.
33. *Raurava Āgama, Upodghāta,* v. 2; Vol. I, p. 1.

34. Ibid., vv. 3-5, p. 1.
35. Ibid., v.8; p.2: "*sarvakṛtsarvavettāraṁ sarvajñānamaparājitam/ sarvabhūtātmabhūtasthaṁ praṇato 'smi sadāśivaṃ* "Sadāśiva" is comparable to the Vaiṣṇavite "Vasudeva"; for a discussion of Vasudeva see H. Brunner-Lauchaux, *SŚP*, p. 10 and the index, p. 335.
36. *Raurava Āgama, Śivatattvāni*, v. 14. p. 5: "*tato 'dhiṣṭhāya vidyeśo māyāṁ sa parameśvaraḥ/kṣobhayitvā svakiraṇaiḥ sṛjate taijasīm kalāṃ*"
37. cf. v. 51B-52, and *MK*, v. 117. For the contra "*ekatva*" see *TS*, v. 54 and *MK*, vv. 131-133. The liberated condition of *Vidyeśvaras* is a lower type of liberation. The higher *mokṣa* is the "*Śivasāmya*" wherein all the bonds are removed and the soul's "*dṛk-kriyā-śakti*" becomes manifest. Aghora Śiva is emphatic that this (*Śiva-*) *samyārūpa* is not a participation in a condition of "oneness" in the way represented by a "universal", i.e., the soul does not come to participate in "śivahood". Rather, it is a more negative condition wherein every distinction between the soul and Śiva "falls away".
38. Raurava Āgana (vidyāpāda), V.I.18.
39. Bhāskarī, p.xii.
40. Gonda, Medieval Religious Literature, p. 215.
41. These four traditionally accepted "*anubandha*" (eg., *tatra anubandho nāma adhikārivișayasambandhaprayojanāni* – Sadānanda's *Vedāntasāra*, 1.5) are not always clearly evident in the original texts as interpreted by the commentators; for example, Kumāril Bhaṭṭa in the *pratijñānasūtram*, 11-25 of his *Ślokavārttika* draws all four from Jaimini's first sūtra, "*athāto dharmajijñāsā*".
42. By "logic" Sadyojyoti is referring to something along the lines which includes "simple enumeration" (*uddeśa*), definition (*lakṣaṇa*) and examination (*parīkṣā*), which are considered to be the characteristics good manuals (*Saṁgraha*) should possess; see, for example, Athalye's notes in the *Tarka Saṁgraha of Annaṁbhaṭṭa with Author's Dīpikā* and Goverdhana's *Nyāya Bodhinī*, ed. by Y. V. Athalye and trans. by M. R. Bodas, 2nd ed., Bombay Sanskrit Series, No. LV (Poona: Bhandarkar Institute Press, 1963), p. 71.
43. This is the same claim made by Ruru in the *RĀ*; in fact, many *Āgamic* authors claim that the material they are presenting is a condensed version of a larger and more detailed teaching.
44. Aghora Śiva takes the term "*sādhakāḥ*" to refer to the "*ācāryāḥ*" by playing on the etymology of the term "*sādhaka*"; the "*ācāryāḥ*" are

the ones who "bring to accomplishment" (*sādhayanti*) both *bhoga* and *mokṣa.* Aghora Śiva's comments do not, however, agree with Sadyojyoti's own remark at the end of the *MK* that the work was written for the "dull minded" (*mandabuddhi*).

Concerning the term "*sādhaka*" in the *Āgama,* H. Brunner-Lauchaux defines the term in its technical usage in light of the four scales of Āgamic Saivite initiation, i.e., *samayin, putraka, sādhaka* and *ācārya.* The *sādhaka* "is the disciple who, after the initiations called *samaya* and *nirvāṇa-dīkṣā,* chooses the path of powers (*siddhi*) and is given to that effect a special consecration." see "*Le Sādhaka,* Personnage oublié du sivaïsme du sud," *Année,* 1975, p. 443.

Generally, *samayadīkṣā* and *viśeṣadīkṣā* allow one to worship Śiva, render service in the temples and observe obligatory duty. "But the *nirvāṇadīkṣā* is one which provides eligibility for the study, reflection etc. of the *Āgamas.*" See *ŚPB,* p. 297. The *ŚPB* lists seven different kinds of *dīkṣā,* although it does not discuss *ācāryābhiṣeka.*

45. "*Bhoga*" as "enjoyment" also has reference to karma, as the soul is the one who enjoys the effects of karmic fruits. "*Anurañjika*" is also etymologically used in describing *rāga*; the soul is "affected/ coloured by raga" (*rāgena rañjitaḥ*), which designates the attachement to objects (*viṣaya-āsaktiḥ* or *viṣaya anurañjakam*). In Sāṁkhya the term has the same sense; for example, in his commentary on *SK* 40, Gauḍapāda glosses "to be endowed with" (*adhivāsita*) [with respect to the subtle body being endowed with the eight *bhāvas*] with "*anurañjita*".

46. Although a distinction must be drawn between the three fundamental categories or "*padārthas*"—i.e. *pati, paśu* and *pāśa*—and the concept of the tattvas, quite often even the *padārathas* are referred to as *tattvas.* In the *Ratna Traya* and *Tattva Traya,* for instance, the three basic "*tattvas*" that are discussed are actually the three *padārthas* (in the former work, *bindu* is representative of *pāśa* while in the latter *māyā* is). According to the *Tattva-Traya Nirṇaya* the three *padārthas* are said to be aspatial, atemporal and possessed of agentive powers. In his commentary on *BK* 145B Aghora Śiva uses the term "*tattva*" to describe a "*padārtha*". There is also an unresolved problem over which *padārtha* the five Pure Tattvas (*Śiva, Śakti, Sadāśiva, Īśvara, Mantreśa,* and *Sadvidyā-mantra*)

should fall. On the one hand, qua *tattvas*, they are said to fall under the *pati-padārtha* while, on the other hand, as "*higher*" forms of *māyā* (i.e., and *bindu*) they are said to fall under the *pāśa-padārtha.*

Different texts assume more than three *padārthas;* Śivāgrayogin enumerates the various extra *padārthas* held by other *Āgamas,* but concludes that the extra *tattvas* fall under the *pāśapadārtha.* Cf. *ŚPB,* pp. 59-60; as well, see Das gupta, p. 29 and *MPĀ*, xviii-xxiv.

47. The second *sūtra* of the *Yoga Sūtras* states the importance of this concept in terms of the goal of yogic practice: "*yogaścittavṛttinirodhaḥ*".

TRANSLATION

Aghora Śiva's Commentary on Sadyojyoti's Bhoga Kārikā

TRANSLATION[1]

Aghora Śiva's Commentary on Sadyojyoti's Bhoga Kārikā

(Manual Concerning Mundane-Experience)

Having made obeisance to Śiva, who is the giver of felicitous mundane-experience (*bhoga*) and release, I am going to explain the *Bhoga Kārikā* very briefly and clearly for the benefit of the slow minded.

Before the venerable Sadyojyoti begins his verses that explicate the nature of mundane-experience and release, he first makes obeisance to the supreme Śiva for the unhampered completion of this work:

> (1) I first make obeisance to the unborn and unchanging Śiva who knows all three times and all the events occurring therein. Śiva grants both mundane-experience and release. Mundane-experience occurs when the triadically bound souls are yoked to *kalā;* release arises through the separation from mundane-experience.[2]

The three bonds are of the nature of *mala, karma* and *māyā.* Those who are possessed by these three bonds are the conscious souls called "*sakalas*", who have this "contact with *kalā*". This contact involves the connection to the constitutive parts of *māyā,* i.e., *māyā* in the form of the bodies born with their respective worlds and in the constitutive structure of the tattvas constituting the subtle body, (i.e., the tattvas beginning with *kalā* and ending with earth). Śiva grants mundane-experience by means of this connection and release through the separation from it.

Śiva's omniscience and ability to confer grace on all beings is indicated by the very fact of His eternal state of release; likewise, He "knows all three times and all the events occurring therein", i.e., He knows all the things that take place in their respective times and the lapses of times of all the living beings. As Śiva is without impurity (*mala*) and is omnipotent, He is necessarily omniscient concerning all time. As well, since Śiva is without impurity, He is "unborn", i.e., without the birth which is characterized by the connection to a body. The term "unchanging" in the verse means "to be unchangeable", i.e., not to be subject to change, like *bindu* etc., as change entails materiality.

Continuing the first verse, he says:

(2) For the purpose of the adepts, I am briefly describing both mundane-experience and release along with their means as they are propounded in the teachings of Ruru and as they are established through perfect logical argumentation.

"The Adepts" are the "teachers" and so fourth, who can explicate the basic principles of both mundane-experience and release. The author is going to describe both mundane-experience and release as they are established in the *Raurava Āgama;* he is also going to employ "logical argumentation", i.e., inferential reasoning, in order that the teachers may better explain the means [of mundane-experience and release] for initiatory purposes and so forth.

In order to clarify the nature of mundane-experience and the means whereby it is brought about, he now describes the ones who are qualified for it:

(3) The lust for mundane-experience arises in accordance with the karmic accumulations of those souls who, because of their defilement and so forth, have been driven into the cycle of worldly existence by God.[3]

"The lust for mundane-experience" refers to "the desire

for mundane-experience" that arises in accordance with the karmic predispositions applicable to wordly existence. This condition of mundane-experience is caused solely by the defilement – i.e., by the *mala* – of those souls who have been driven into mundane-experience through the superintendence of God (i.e., Śiva) acting through the instrumentality of Ananta etc.

Sāṁkhya raises the objection that the soul is without *mala*. But this is false since a soul without *mala* cannot be subject to mundane-experience.[4] Moreover, if it is possible for a soul without *mala* to be attached to mundane-experience, this attachment can also arise in the case of the released soul.

Sāṁkhya objects: the attachment to mundane-experience is a result of the connection to passion (*rāga*). True! But even in the case of passion, the cause of the attachment is simply due to those who have *mala*![5] In this respect, the *Svāyambhuva Āgama* states: "If the soul were not defiled, how could its attachment to mundane-experience ever come about?"

He now addresses the question concerning the nature and means of mundane-experience:

> (4) As the desirous-attachment to the modifications of the mind (*buddhi-vṛtti*), mundane-experience is brought about by the various means which themselves are a product of the primal material cause of the world into which the will of god has entered.[6]

"God" is understood in this verse as Ananta, the only one who can agitate *māyā*. The *Kiraṇa Āgama* states: Śiva is declared to be the agent in the pure realm while Ananta is the Lord in the bound realm.[7] Ananta's desire causes the agitation of the primal material cause of the world, which is called "*māyā*"; mundane-experience arises through the "means" (*sadhana*) which have been engendered on account of this agitation of *māyā*. The "means" are [threefold]: a) of the nature of the subtle bodies that are of a restricted character [i.e., restricted to particular souls];

b) of the nature of worlds that are common [i.e., shared by different souls]; and c) of the nature of bodies born with worlds, which is both a restricted and common condition.[8]

Mundane-experience is here understood to be of the nature of the attachment to the modifications of the mind (*buddhi-vṛtti*); more specifically, mundane-experience is the "attachment" of the sentient soul to the modifications of the mind. The mind is of the nature of the cognition (*adhyavasāya*) constituted by pleasure, suffering and delusion. The "attachment", which is of a desirous nature, relates to the condition of the modifications of the mind whose cognitive structure (*adhyavasāya-ākāra*) is constituted by pleasure. This attachment is an awareness (*saṁvitti*) [on the part of the soul] best described as "direct experience" (*anubhava*) that is not of the nature of a "reflection" (*pratibimba*); the reflection [of the mind on the soul] allows change to be attributed to the soul. Thus, the *Svāyambuva Āgama* states: "mundane-experience is the [bound] soul's experience, which is characterized by pleasure, suffering etc."

With respect to the gross elements, he is now going to discuss the means whereby mundane-experience is brought about:

> (5) "Filled out" by means of the increase of their respective subtle elements, [the gross elements] earth, water, fire, air and ether bring about the constitutive structure [of mundane-experience] through their [respective] qualities, functional modifications and sense organs.

Herein, just the qualities etc. of the gross elements establish the existence of the gross elements as constituents of mundane-experience. The qualities are odour etc. The functional modifications are "bearing" etc. "Serving as the support of the sense-organs" means "serving as that which bears the sense organs". The sense organs will be explained in the sequel.

The meaning of the verse therefore is: the earth and so

forth, by means of their qualities and functions and by means of bearing the sense-organs, become engaged in the means whereby mundane-experience arises for the [bound] souls. Of what [source] are the earth and so forth? He says: "Of the filling out" by means of the "increasing" of their respective subtle elements. The "filling out" (*puṣṭāna*) arises on account of the "increasing" (*pūraṇa*) that is a condition of "becoming full" that occurs by means of the subtle elements, which are themselves the material causes (*kāraṇabhūta*) [of earth etc.]. The activity of *prakṛti* is [likewise said to have two functions]: "the increasing of that which has already been accomplished and the acting as the means of that which has not yet been accomplished".[9] Through a gross and subtle condition, the gross elements with their causes, which are the subtle elements, act as the conditions supporting the organs.[10] The *Mataṅga Āgama* states: the subtle elements are like a pot and the gross elements like its covering. It is said: this tenfold effect [i.e., the gross elements and subtle elements], having entered into the condition of supporting the organs, causes the activity of the organs. On the other hand, since the organs lack their own power to act, they are only active after they come to depend on the support of the effect.[11]

When the general function of the gross elements exists, the specific functions–i.e., bearing etc.–exist as well. Having their locus in the subtle body, the gross elements share a "common" function consisting in the property of "increasing" which takes place by means of the body as it is understood in its essential sense as a "covering over" [*diha,* etymological sense of *deha,* body], i.e., an "increasing". This property of increasing belongs to the gross elements as they come to take their locus (*sthāna*) in the external body. When this common function exists, the gross elements' specific function, e.g., supporting, etc., exists as well.

He says:

(6) When the earth etc. constitute the body and serve as

> the locus for the sense-organs, the activities of the earth etc. are supporting, bringing together, maturing, structuring and providing space.[12]

The function of the earth is "supporting" (*dhṛti*), which is a "bearing" (*dhāraṇa*). The function of water is "bringing together" (*saṁgraha*), which is a "binding" (*avaṣṭambha*). The function of fire is "maturing" (*pakti*), which is a "ripening" (*pāka*). Air has the function of ("structuring") (*vyūha*), which is a "joining of parts" (*avayavaghaṭana*). Ether (*ākāśa*) has the function of "providing" (*dāna*) space (*avakāśa*), which is the providing of a "receptacle" (*āspada*). He will now describe the gross elements' common function i.e., "the supporting of the sense-organs" (*indriya-ādhāratva*) which takes place through the locus of the subtle body:

> (7-8Aa) By having its locus in the "transference body", the "instrument" (*karaṇa*) takes on activities and as well travels from one womb to another in order to obtain mundane-experience for souls on account of the imperceptible force [of karma] that provides the appropriate experiences for [the individual] souls.

The "transference body" is the "subtle body": by means of mundane-experience, the *karma* of souls "is caused to be transferred over" (*ativāhayati*), i.e., "is caused to be driven away".[13] Solely in the condition of having its locus in this subtle body is the "instrument" —the collection of organs— active (*ceṣṭate*). It is said: since anything lacking its own power to act cannot be active when it has no supporting-locus (*nirāśraya*), the collection of instruments is active solely through the support (*ādhāra*)of the gross elements and subtle elements[14], which have their locus in the subtle body.[15] Moreover, yielding the appropriate experiences for the individual souls, *karma* causes the instrument that has its locus in the subtle body to travel from one womb to another in order to obtain mundane-experience for those souls possessing this *karma.* In this respect, the *Tattva Saṁgraha* states: the group of *tattvas* beginning with the earth and ending with *kalā* is bound to individual souls; on account of *karma,* such souls wander through all the different worlds in bodies born of those worlds.[16]

On account of being subtle, like the spirits (*piśāca*) etc., the subtle body is not perceivable by us; however, it is experienced through the perception of yogins:

(8Ab-8b) Like the spirits,[17] the transference body, which is the locus of the senses, cannot be experienced through the senses by those who lack lordly powers.

He now describes the qualities of the gross elements:[18]

(9) Odour is in earth;[19] taste is six-fold in earth, but sweetness is confined to earth and water alone; colour belongs to earth, water and fire, being bright in fire, shining in water and of different hues in earth.

(10) This is the arrangement with regard to touch: in both earth and air it is neither hot nor cold,[20] the difference is that one is born from maturing, one not so born; in water it is cool and in fire hot.

(11) As produced from substances derived from sound, sound exists in the lowest four gross elements; in space it is of the collocation of echoes. This is the correct opinion set forth by the wise.

Odour is in earth solely in the form of the fragrant and non-fragrant. Taste is in water and earth. Of the forms of taste that are in water, namely pungency, sourness, saltiness, sweetness, astringency, and bitterness, only sweetness is in earth. Colour is in earth, water and fire etc. In earth, colour is of manifold types: white, red, yellow, black; in water, however, it is only of a shiny colour. In fire it is bright.

The condition of touch is in the airs. In both the earth and air it is neither cold nor hot. What then is the difference between the two touches in earth and air? He says: the difference is that one is born from maturing, one not so born. The touch in earth arises from maturing whereas the one in air does not arise from maturing—this is the difference. Because of this designation [between the two types of touch qualities], colour etc., which are qualities of earth, are only born from maturing. The natural touch of water is just cool and in fire just hot.

Sound arises in the four gross elements—earth etc.—by means of the mutual "clashing together" of their respective substances, ground, etc.;[21] in space, however, sound is of the nature of an echo.

Now, the Vaiśeṣikas raise an objection:[22] sound is established as the special quality of ether, on account of the cognition of it elsewhere than in its locus.[23]

This is false because of the fallacy of 'the passage in time' (*kālātyayāpadiṣṭatva*),[24] as the reason (*hetu*) contradicts both perception and the Āgamic tradition. Thus, sound is solely heard in the locus of sound, as in the drum etc. Moreover, sound is perceived in the earth as the sound of "rubbing together" etc.; in water as a swishing sound etc. (chalacchalādi); in fire as a blowing sound etc.; in air as rustling etc.; and in space it is of the nature of an echo. The argument that sound is the special quality of ether is refuted in detail by us in the *Mṛgendravṛttidīpikā*. It is further stated in the *Mṛgendra Āgama:* sound is in the five gross elements and touch is in four. The neither cold nor hot [touch] is in the earth and air; hot and cold are in water and fire. Brightness is in fire, whiteness in water and a variety [of colours] such as whiteness etc. in earth. Colour is in the three. Taste in water is sweet and is six-fold in the earth. By the wise, odour is considered to be both fragrant and non-fragrant in the earth. (V.I. 12. 27-29).

He sums up what has been said:

(12A-12Ba) Thus described, the earth etc. are generally possess accepted to possess the collection of odour etc.

It is generally accepted that the earth etc. exist as the loci of odour. It is said: the five subtle elements are established as the "cause" (*kāraṇatā*) of the five gross elements, since the five gross elements are established as "effects", which are discerned by means of the external sense-organs of beings like us. He says:

(12Bb) The subtle elements are inferred by means of them.

Thus, the cognition (*grahaṇa*) of a quality (*guṇa*) entails the cognition of the thing that possesses the quality, since there can be no distinction (*avyatirekitva*) [between the quality and the thing possessing it]. He will prove that the qualities of the gross elements do not have a separate existence:

(13) Earth etc. are said to be inherently variegated and manifested by means of their qualities; earth etc. are revealed in a successive manner, just as the painted picture on a cloth that is covered over.

In this verse, the earth and so forth are described. This is the sense: the mutual distinctions are discerned by means of the qualities of odour etc. and the inherent variegations are seen by means of the differences in the phenomenal appearance (*ākāra*) of the ground, stones, mountains, rivers, oceans, etc. Thus, earth etc., are revealed in a successive manner as a painted cloth that is covered over [is revealed in a successive manner]. It is not possible to grasp simultaneously both the respective distinctions and differences in the constitutions that belong to the earth etc., as it is impossible to grasp everything at the same time which is both close at hand and far away. But this can only be revealed in a successive manner by means of inference and the senses. What results from this? He says:

(14) Due to the reason that they are manifested in a successive manner, the earth etc. come within the scope of the cognitive distinctions based on a designation of "the thing qualified" *(viśeṣya)* and "the qualifying thing" *(viśeṣaṇa)*.

The earth etc., on account of being revealed in a successive manner, acquire the status of "objects" of sense (*viṣayatā*) in terms of the designation of their relations (*bhāvavyapadeśa*), i.e., in terms of the cognitive distinctions based on the distinctions of the qualified thing and the qualifying thing, as in such cognitions as: "this earth is fragrant". Thus, he states:

> (15-16A) No cognition of earth is possible without a cognition of odour etc., while a cognition of water etc. takes place without a cognition [of odour etc.]; consequently, earth is separate from water etc. but is not separate from odour etc.

There can never be a cognition of the earth – a "qualified thing" in the form of a possessor of qualities (*dharmi-rūpa*) —without a grasping of the qualities odour etc. – qualifying things (*viśeṣaṇa*); however, even when odour etc. are not grasped in the other elements (water etc.), a cognition [of the earth]still arises. Therefore, for this reason, earth is not separate from odour etc., although separate from water etc. Likewise, the same reasoning applies to the other gross elements:

> (16B) By the wise, the same reasoning should be applied to water etc.

An objection is raised:[25] when beside a porcelain rose, a quartz crystal is apprehended as possessing redness – without the apprehension of its quality as "clear" (*śaukla*). Therefore, [the principle that] the apprehension of the thing possessed by qualities is preceded by the apprehension of the qualities (*guṇigrahaṇasya guṇa-grahaṇa-pūrvakatva*), is unestablished; thus, he says:

> (17) Nor is the inferential mark *(hetu)* we are using here inapplicable in the case of the crystal that is cognized apart from its own colour and which is the colour of a neighbouring object, because colour is not only a matter of hue *(varṇa)* but includes the general configuration *(saṁsthāna)* as well.

Herein the quality (*guṇa*) "colour" – which substances possess – is held to be of the nature of a "configuration" (*saṁsthāna*) possessing "hue" (*varṇa*); therefore, even when one is cognisant of the crystal next to the red porcelain rose, one remembers one's past cognition of the crystal's constitutive "configuration" as circular, four-cornered, etc. along with a memory of the cognition of the crystal's clear hue. Thus, the principle that "the apprehension of the thing possessed by qualities is preceded by the apprehension of the qualities" is established; hence, the inferential mark (*hetu*) is not falsely established.

Having established the ancillary nature of the gross elements in the act of muṇdane-experience, he will demonstrate that the gross elements are "effects" (*kāryatva*) – although without supplying a specific rule (*anirdeśa*) – in order to further qualify the establishment of the subtle elements according to the proposition that "the subtle elements are inferred by means of the gross elements [v. 12Bb]":

> (18) The inferential mark *(hetu)* establishing the fact that the qualities are effects is also fit to establish the fact that the sphere of tattvas beginning with earth and ending with *kalā* have a cause.

It is said: on account of the condition of manifoldness (*anekatva*)in the case of the qualities (*guṇa*), which are of a non-conscious nature, a condition of the priority of the cause (*kāraṇa-pūrvakatva*) exists, as in the case of a pot etc. Thus, solely by means of this inferential mark the earth etc. are established as effects (*kāryatva*). It is said that the subtle body, which is restricted to individual souls, is of the nature of thirty *tattvas* beginning with the earth and ending with *kalā*, on account of the failure to establish anything else to account for the variety (*vaicitrya*) of mundane-experience as it is manifested. The *Āgamas* state that the priority of the cause is established on account of the manifoldness that exists when there is the condition or unconsciouness occurring by means of those *tattvas* (earth etc.) restricted to individual souls.

The successiveness (*krama*) of the earth etc. is established solely on account of the distinctions between their respective qualities, i.e., on account of the establishment of the subtle elements as the causes of the gross elements. He says:

(19) By possessing one more of sound etc., the subtle elements exceed one another in a graduated order. Since they lack characteristic qualities, the subtle elements are established as the successively operating generating causes of earth etc., which possess qualities.

This is the meaning of the verse: the material cause of ether is the subtle element sound, whose natural condition is just the sound that has the character of being unmanifest; proceeding one step lower, the material cause of air is the subtle element touch, whose natural condition is just of the nature of sound and touch. The material cause of fire is the subtle element colour, whose natural condition is just of the nature of sound, touch and colour.[26] The material cause of water is the subtle element taste, which is just of the nature of sound, touch, colour and taste. The material cause of earth is the subtle element odour, which is of the nature of the five qualities beginning with sound and ending with odour.

"By possessing one more of sound etc., the subtle elements exceed one another in a graduated order" means that there is an increase of the qualities (*guṇādhikya*), i.e., a sequential increase by one (*ekottara*) of sound etc., which are possessed by ether etc. "Since they lack characteristic qualities, the subtle elements..." means that the subtle elements are not characterized by qualities, i.e., they belong to the group of sound etc., which is of a nonmanifest nature. On this account, the subtle elements sound etc. are the successively-operating "generating causes" – i.e., the material causes of the ether etc. The subtle elements endeavor to establish the gradual ordering to the manifestation (*sṛṣṭi-krama*) of the gross element, ether etc., which, as the substrata of qualities, possess the manifested qualities. The subtle elements engage in "the condition of going lower and lower by means of the successive increase of the qualities"; this means that the subtle elements cause the condition of going "lower and lower" even in the case of the "effects".

Again, how do the subtle elements contribute as ancillaries in the act of mundane-experience? He says:

(20) As the generating causes of all things, the subtle elements contain the causative factor involved in the genesis of its own effect and of its own increasing–this is the means whereby the aim of the soul *(pumartha)* is accomplished.

The constituents involved in the act of mundane-experience on the one hand act as the means of that which has not yet been accomplished and on the other hand facilitate the increase of that which has already been accomplished. In other words, the constitutive nature of mundane-experience is established both (a) on account of the condition that generates the means whereby mundane-experience is effected, which involves the generating causes of the effects (i.e., *māyā* etc.) and the subtle elements and (b) by means of the condition that increases this effect.

In order to describe the constitutive elements involved in the act of mundane-experience with respect to the sense-organs, he first establishes the motor organs:

(21) The genitals, feet, anus, mouth and hands are distinct from the activities: delight, movement, evacuation, speaking, and grasping.

Evacuation is the release of bodily excretions. The verse states that the organs of action, genitals etc., are established on the basis of the activities of delight etc.

An objection is raised: the organs are just these [physical] loci, the genitals etc.!

This is not the case, as he says:

(22) Even in the presence of a given body part there may be the absence of a given activity. The entity upon which the absence or presence of the actual activity depends is thus the motor organ, and not just the body part alone.

The activity of movement etc. is not seen to occur without

the respective capacity of the [motor] organ, even though there is the presence of some physical condition, such as the feet etc. Therefore, even when the given body parts exist, the activities of the body parts are dependent for their absence or presence on the existence of the capacities, i.e., the five organs, which are separate [from the body parts]. Thus, only in this manner are the motor organs established and the position of the Naiyāyikas and others rejected.

An objection is raised: the motor organs must be considered to be innumerable due to the activity of raising the eyebrows etc.[27]

He responds:

> (23) The motor organs have been established by means of the activities of delight etc. Therefore, the claim that the motor organs are innummerable cannot be accepted on account of the activities.

It would be false for us to hold that motor organs are functions of parts of the body. As in the case of the sense of touch wherein it is established that this sense pervades the body, so it is in the case of the [motor organ] "hand" whose activity is inclusive of "raising of the eyebrows, etc."[28] As well, "the activity of evacuation" belongs [in all parts of the body] to [what is designated as] the anus. On account of the distinctions entailed by the inherent characteristics of delight etc.–even in the case of raising of eyebrows etc.–the innumerableness of the organs cannot be established. In sum, there is no inconsistency in holding (a) that there are only five motor organs due to the existence of the [five] primary activities, described as delight etc. and (b) that the respective designations of the motor organs are not innumerable, since the special locus of the motor organs is in various places.

He will now establish the sense-organs:

> (24) In the grasping of sound etc. the activity of the agent–i.e., the soul–is not without a [sense] organ *(karaṇa)*;

moreover, there cannot be just one organ, as a necessary requirement for another would not cease.

Without an organ the activity of grasping sound etc. would not arise, just as the activity of "chopping" would not arise without an axe. Moreover, these five activities do not arise solely on account of one organ as hearing etc; for, in this case, the requirement for another organ would not cease. For example, when there is the sense of hearing, which is the organ in the grasping of sound, there is a necessary requirement for different organs–the sense of touch etc.– when there is the grasping of touch etc. This is the meaning of the verse.

Exactly what are the organs? In answer, he says:

(25A) The organs are [designated by]:ear,skin, eye, tongue, and nose.

The organs are inferred by means of the inability to bring forth anything else to explain [the particular sense-organ restrictiveness of] the grasping of sound etc.; accordingly, he says:

(25B) The function of these organs lies in the perceiving *(ālocana)* of sound etc. when in the proximity *(saṁnidhi)* of sound etc.[29]

If we were to take the reading of "like" (*saṁnibha*) [in place of "proximity" (*saṁnidhi*)], the meaning of this half of the verse would be: the sense-organs that are superintended over by *manas,* together with the mind, the ascertaining faculty (*adhyavasāyin*), supply the *vidyā tattva* with its objects, i.e., the internal 'forms' (*ākāra*) that resemble the external "forms" of sound etc. In the sequel we will describe how the soul apprehends things through the organ designated "*vidyā*" that is in association with the content of the cognitive activity of the mind, which has been presented with material from the senses. It is stated elsewhere: the soul is conscious of objects that have been cognitively ascertained by the mind.

It is not the case that the sense-organs are simply the physical loci (*sthāna*), such as the auditory passage of the ear etc. The sense-organs are "conditions" of certain "capacities" (*śakti*). The cognition of sound etc. does not arise when there is a defect (due to karmic influences) in the capacity of the physical loci. He says:

(26) Do not think that the body parts alone are the sense-organs because even when there is the presence of the body parts there can be an absence of cognition due to some defect.

He now discusses the internal organ (*antaḥkaraṇa*):

(27) Cognition (*bodha*), active-effort (*saṁrambha*) and will (*icchā*) cannot be brought about by the various means of mundane-experience that have already been discussed. Rather, they are brought about by means of the internal organs: the mind (*buddhi*), ego (*ahaṃkāra*) and *manas.*

The means whereby 'will' etc. are accomplished are the internal instruments–mind, ego and *manas.* One is led to this conclusion for three reasons: 1) the *tattvas* beginning with earth are established solely by means of their effects [i.e., mind, ego and *manas*]; 2) there is no way to prove that there is some other reason or reasons to explain the effects; and 3) it is not possible to postulate a manifold number of *tattvas* [*to* account for the effects].[30] The term "will" refers to "volition" (*saṃkalpa*); as the function of *manas,* volition is of the nature of sequential attentiveness. "Effort" is the "exertion" (*prayatna*) of the ego; "cognition" is the "ascertainment" (*adhyavasāya*) carried out by the mind. All this will be explained in the sequel.

The means whereby the purpose of the soul (*puruṣārtha*) is accomplished takes place through the mutual assistance of the internal and external organs. He says:

(28-29) As in the case of the palanquin and the palanquin bearers, the internal and external organs combine together to accomplish the activity of willing etc.; if there is an absence of either the accomplishment of "inward activities" or the cognitions directed toward external objects, the activity of willing etc., which is for the purpose of [the soul's] consciousness, does not arise.

The internal and external organs, like the palanquin and the palanquin bearers, together become the means whereby the activities of willing etc. are accomplished. This is so for two reasons. First, ascertainment and so forth are seen to occur only when there is a prior perception of external objects. Secondly, it is impossible to apprehend an external object without attentiveness etc. Consequently, when there is the loss of either collection of the external organs of sound etc. or of the internal organs (i.e., of "the accomplishment of the inward activities") neither the activities of willing etc. nor the cognitions of external objects such as sound etc. can arise as providing the means of accomplishing the purpose of the soul (the phrase "for the purpose of consciousness" means "for the purpose of the soul" and is employed to refer to mundane-experience). Analogously, when there is the absence either of the palanquin or the palanquin bearers, the activity of "bearing" is not observed.

He now addresses the position of an opponent:

(30A) Others establish the "life-force" *(prāṇa)* as the internal organ and as that which manifests consciousness.

"Others" refers to one school of the materialists who claim that the internal organ is simply "air" (*vāyu*) designated by the term "life-force". This life-force manifests consciousness as a property which is a result of the transformation of the elements (*bhūta-pariṇāma-viśeṣa*); the life-force is the cause of sentient existence etc. through the functions of "taking up" etc. He points out the falsity of this view:

(30B) Without volitional activities, there is no life-force. But then what is the organ of the volitional activities?

Behavioral activity (*pravṛtti*) is indeed seen to be preceded by volitional activity (*prayatna*) on account of the intermittence of the air that is of the nature of the life-force. It is said: how can there be the drawing out of activity (*preraṇākarṣa*) without the volitional activity of air? The internal organ is consequently established in response to the question: in the establishment of volitional activity, which is of the nature of "active effort", how should the organ be conceived? Moreover, if it is claimed that the production of consciousness as well arises from this air, another organ ought to be brought forward to account for this production:

(31) The task of manifesting consciousness is attributed to this life-force. However, describe its internal organ! As well, belonging to the life-force, consciousness can never become manifest, because air is like the external wind.

It is not correct to argue that the manifestation of consciousness can belong to something unconscious (*jaḍa*), as this would result in the claim that the manifestation of consciousness can belong to everything. Consciousness does not belong to this air [qua life-force], because air is like the air that is external [to the body].

Thus having refuted the claim that the life-force is the internal organ, he now discusses the role of *manas* as one of the three forms of the internal instrument already mentioned.

(32) *Manas* is postulated as the cause of the will *(icchā-hetu)*. It functions rapidly and prompts the external organs into action. Because it functions so rapidly, the cognitions of the agent cannot take place simultaneously.

The term employed in this verse to refer to the sense organs [i.e., *deva*] is so used because the sense-organs "shine" (*devana*), i.e., they "illuminate" things.[31] The word "cognitions" in the verse refers to those cognitions that are characterized as having this or that object. Even when the soul is in association with the senses and their objects, the sense-organs do not function simultaneously; in no way can this ever happen.[32] *Manas* prompts the external sense-organs, causes the attention (*avadhāna*) that is of the nature of volition (*saṁkalpa*), i.e., "will" (*icchā*) and acts as the "organ" for behavioral activity (*pravṛtti*). It is said: the controlling factor (*adhikārin*) is twofold: it superintends (*adhiṣṭhāna*) over the external organs and it internally superintends over the internal organ, i.e., the volitional activity of pleasure etc. The *Mataṅga Āgama* states: the twofold controlling factor is the consciousness (*citta* [i.e., *manas*] that causes the mundane-experience of the mundane-experiencer; one part always exists by [the control over] the external organs under its control and the other part exists by its own activity, i.e., by volition (*saṁkalpa*). *Manas* provides the capacity (*sāmarthya*) of the sense-organs with an internal locus (*antaḥsthita*); for this reason, it is considered to be an internal organ.[33] The *Mṛgendra Āgama* also states: *manas* is possessed of the rapid activity that prompts the sense-organs into action and is characterized by volition.[34]

An objection is raised: five cognitions are seen to arise simultaneously when there is a nice murmuring sound[35] while one is eating a cake that is very large, pleasing to look at, and pleasant to smell.

No, this is not the case! The five cognitions arise solely in an indistinguishable and imperceptible sequentiality, like the perforation that is made in the hundred lotus leaves [by a needle][36]. Thus, it is said that *manas* "functions rapidly".

He now established the ego:

(33A-33Bb) As a function of the ego, "effort" prompts air (with its five functions) to sustain life.

"To sustain life" means "for the purpose of sustaining the body." The "five functions" are bringing forward (*praṇayana*), discharging (*apanayana*), etc.; by means of their respective functions (*vṛtti*), they acquire the designations of life-force (*prāṇa*), respiration (*apāna*), etc.

As a function of the ego "effort", i.e., "exertion" (*prayatna*) prompts air into activity. Thus is the ego established.

The *Mṛgendra Āgama* states: as an organ of the soul the ego arises from the mind, which is from something other than the manifest [i.e., the *guṇas*]; by the ego's effort (*saṁrambha*) etc., the five airs of the body become active.[37] The activity of the vital force is "bringing forward" (*praṇayana*), which directs the subtle body either below or upwards. The activity of respiration (*apāna*) is the lower reaching "discharging" (*apanayana*)of excrement etc. The activity of generality (*samāna*) is the "distributing" (*nayana*) of the nutrients (*rasarūpa*) of food etc. throughout the body. The activity of the diffused air (*vyāna*) is the "bending" (*vinamana*) of the limbs of the body. The activity of "breathing upwards" (*udāna*) is the "raising" (*unnayan*) of interior sound into articulate sound (*varṇatā*). Thus, the essentials of the five activities have been discussed. Since it is said that the agency of *udgāra* (expelling) etc. belongs to air (*vāyu*), the *Kālottara Āgama* says: in eructation, *nāga* is emitted; in the activity of opening the eyes, it is *kūrma* that is present; in sneezing it is *kṛkara;* in yawning it is *Devadatta;* in nourishment (*poṣa*), it is the acquisition of wealth, which is not abandoned even at death.[38]

Furthermore, the activity (*vṛtti*) that specifically belongs to the ego concerns the conception (*pratyaya*) that is of the nature of an ascertainment (*adhyavasāya*) of the cognizer, as in "I am", which remains the same throughout the cognitions of all objects. There is a complete difference between this kind of conception and the one that is a result of the mind (*buddhi-kārya*) in the form of an ascertainment of an object that is grasped; this conception remains separate (*bhinna-rūpa*) for each object. He says:

> (33Bb) The other is that which is different from the conception of an object.

This means: the conception that is of the nature of the activity of the ego is different from the conception of an object. An objection is raised: the specific activities of hearing etc. are the grasping of sound etc.; since the common activity of these sense-organs is "effort", why postulate something else, i.e., the ego.? Hence, he says:

> (34) Effort (*saṃrambha*) cannot be established as the common activity of the sense-organs because even when there is a defect in one of the sense-organs, the ego continues to function.

The effect (*kārya*) that specifically belongs to the ego is either the conception "I am" or the effort that exists even when there is a defect in one of the sense-organs, since it is said: when one of the agents responsible for a common effect is not functioning, no activity arises. It follows that the collection of the subtle elements, organs of action, and sense-organs, together with *manas*, arise solely from the ego. He points this out:

> (35) The three divisions of the ego sequentially generate the three groups called *taijasa* etc., which are derived from sattva etc.

The over-abundance of either *sattva, rajas,* or *tamas* sequentially becomes the threefold grouping of either *sāttvika, rājasa* or *tāmasa,* which are designated as *taijasa, vaikārika* and *bhūtādi.* The ego's triadic condition as *sāttvika* etc. is due to the abundance of the *sattva* quality etc. The mixture of the different qualities of the ego's triadic condition arises in accordance with the maxim that "there is no change without mixture."

"What arises and from whence does it arise?" In response to this, he says:

> (36) Since the quality of the sense-organs and *manas* is of an illuminating nature, the sense-organs therefore derive from the ego, which is sāttvika and thus similar to them.

After outlining the Naiyāyika's position, he will refute it:

(37) Others claim that the sense-organs are derived from the gross elements since the reason is unestablished concerning the restriction of the scope [of the sense-organs].

This is what the Naiyāyikas hold: the ear is the sole apprehender of sound, skin the sole apprehender of touch etc. Thus, on account of the restrictedness of the scope of the sense-organs with their respective objects, the sense-organs arise from the gross elements, which are the loci of sound etc.[39] However, if the ego is construed as the cause of the sense-organs, the sense-organs should be of one nature (*eka-rūpa*), since they would be derived from one cause. There would, therefore, be no restrictiveness of the scope of each sense-organ. Thus, the Naiyāyikas think that the reason (*hetu*) is unestablished on account of the unestablishment of the accomplishment of the restrictiveness concerning the material cause (*prakṛti-niyama*) of the sense-organs, i.e., of the restrictiveness concerning their scope.[40] In response: in the case wherein the sense-organs are restricted to a certain [material] scope, the sense-organs should grasp just those gross elements (along with their qualities) which are the material causes of the respective sense-organs. However, the eye etc. grasp different substances and their qualities:

(38) Solely in a non-restrictive manner does the skin, which is related to the wind, grasp the substances along with wind and the four "touches" relating to the four substances.

The sense of touch, which is held to be related to the wind (*vāyavyatva*), grasps the earth, water and fire together with the wind (and the four touches which are related to them). He adds:

(39) Moreover, the sense of sight grasps three substances and the colours in them; consequently, one cannot postulate a [material] restriction concerning the scope of the sense-organs.

He now puts forth another criticism:

(40) If one holds that the restriction of the scope of the sense-organs is due to their origin in the material elements, it will be impossible for persons to have cognition–derived from the senses–of "movement", "general trait", and "intimate union".

When there is the acceptance of a restriction of the scope of the sense-organs, which serves a material purpose, the cognitions arising from the sense-organs concering the categories of "movement", "general trait" and "inherence" —which you accept as distinct from the elements and their qualities–ought not arise.

But how can there be a difference in the senses qua effects when these senses are of the same nature as the ego?

The differences in the senses is thought to be like the arising of differences in the changes of sugar cane in molasses, candy, etc.

When there is a requirement for a restricting factor (*niyāmaka*) in the grasping of sound etc. by the sense of hearing etc., we hold that the restricting factor is just *karma,* which is the bestower of human destiny. He says:

(41) I do not hold that the cause of the restriction arises from the ego; rather, the cause is karma, which is the bestower of human destiny according to the will of Śiva.

We do no hold that the ego is the sole cause in the restriction of the scope [of the sense-organs]; rather, the cause is *karma,* which is superintended over by Śiva – this is the meaning.

If a portion of space circumscribed by an opening in the body makes sound manifest, then it follows that the sense of hearing should as well belong to the nasal cavities! Thus, in the case of the restriction of the grasping of sound, which wholly belongs to the space of the ear, even those who hold that the sense-organs are material maintain that the restricting factor is "*karma*", designated as "the imperceptible factor" (*adṛṣṭa*). He says:

> (42) Due to the fear of postulating many loci of hearing, others as well claim that karma, which is the bestower of that [human destiny], is the cause of the restricting of the mundane-experience of sound to an inherence [in the ether circumscribed by the body].

The sense of the verse is as follows: fearing the postulation of multiple sources of hearing when the apprehension of sound is held to be innate to the ether of the body, you too hold that *karma* (the bestower of human destiny) is the sole cause involved in the restriction of the apprehension of sound as circumscribed by the ether of the ear.

He is now going to discuss the motor organs as arising from the ego:

> (43) Since an effect acts in conformity with its cause, the collection of motor organs, which act as the agents of action, arise from the *vaikārika* [aspect of the ego] which is *rājasa*.

According to the principle that an effect acts in conformity with its cause, the collection of motor organs causing bodily activity arises from the "*vaikārika*" division of the ego; derived from the [abundance of] the guṇa "*rajas*", this division of the ego is referred to as "*rājasa*" and is the cause of activity in general. This same principle applies to the sense-organs: because they are of an illuminating nature, the sense- organs are derived from *sattva*, as illumination is a property of *sattva*.

However, if one holds that the sense and motor organs, which are by nature distinct, arise from a single cause, one commits oneself to the fallacy of infinite regress concerning the non-restrictiveness of the cause. He says:

(44) If it is thought that the arising of both the *sāttvika* group and the *rājasa* group are solely drived from *sattva* then it will be impossible to ward off the logical fault of "infinite regress" *(anavasthā)*.

Thus:

(45) Moreover, as separate from the other two groups and as manifested from *tamas*, the group of subtle elements therefore arises from the [division of ego] called "elemental" *(bhūtādi)*.

He now describes the cause (*hetutva*) of the ascertainment etc. (*adhyavasāyādi*) that belong to the mind:

(46) The modifications of the mind are described as "cognition", since the mind is the locus wherein the [bound] soul's cognition occurs. The mind's cognitive activity is never simply due to the instrumentality of the sense-organs whereby the manifestation that is of the form of the object is manifested.

The particular manifestation (*prakāśa*) that is of the nature of the ascertainment (*adhyavasāya*) of external objects, as in "this is a pot", certainly arises on account of the instrumentality of the sense-organs. However, aside from this, cognition is the specific activity of the mind since it is the locus whereby the soul's cognition is manifested. The manifestation of cognition is said to take place either through "dispositions" and "conceptions" (which will be discussed in the sequel) or else through memory, imagination etc. Thus it is said that the mind is established as having the characteristic of conceptions, memory and etc. The *Mṛgendra Āgama* states: this manifestation of the mind is characterized by dispositions and conceptions. Since it is the locus (*bhūmitā*) of the manifestation of cognition for the bound soul, it is called "cognition"[41]. This mental cognition (*buddhi-bodha*) occurs in three ways; he says:

(47Aa) Imagination *(klṛpti)*, discernment *(mati)* and memory *(smṛti)*.

"Imagination" refers to the imaginative envisioning (*pratibhā*), i.e., the activity of imagining (*kalpanā*).

"Discernment" is the ascertaining activity (*adhyavasāya*), i.e., understanding (*jñāna*) – cognitive activity (*manana*).[42]

He now concludes that the differences of the internal organ are established on account of the differences in the "effects" (*kārya*), such as will etc.

(47ab-47b) Since the effects – which are called will, effort and cognition – designate separate functions, the internal organ is tripartite.

The meaning of the verse is as follows: although these are subordinate distinctions of memory etc., the activity of the mind is still designated as "cognition", since this is the single function of the mind; the activities of will etc. have separate causes, because they have separate functions.

An objection is raised. Let the means whereby mundane-experience arises be attributed to the cause whereby things are apprehended, which [function] belongs to the senses, since the condition of being "an object of mundane experience" is due to the earth etc. becoming objects [of the senses]. The means whereby mundane-experience arises cannot be attributed to the mind; mundane-experience is of the nature of a cognitive experience that arises in the soul on account of the contact between the senses and objects. Moreover, according to the *Naiyāyikas* and others, the mind is only a quality of the soul; he says:

(48) [objection]: But, the "object of cognition" *(samvedya)* is established as something which is a quality of something of like nature; as well, the mind *(buddhi)* is not an "object of cognition" – such is your excellent logic!

The meaning of the verse follows. Cognition is twofold [according to us]: of the nature of ascertainment (*adhyavasāya*) and not of the nature of ascertainment.

Cognition that is not of the nature of an ascertainment exists simply as a "faculty of apprehension" (*grahaka*) which is an eternal and intrinsic characteristic of the soul.[42] Cognition that is of the nature of ascertainment is transitory and is not an intrinsic characteristic of the soul, since it is improper for something intrinsically transitory to be attributed to something intrinsically eternal; thus, cognition qua ascertainment is an intrinsic characteristic of something other than the soul, i.e., the mind. The mind causes the ascertainment of the dispositions and is itself qualified by *dharma, jñāna* etc. As well, the condition of being an "object of cognition" can only belong to the mind, since (a) the mind is an "object of mundane-experience" due to its association with the three guṇas (*sattva* etc.) in the form of the dispositions and conceptions, and since (b) the mind itself is of the nature of the ascertainment of the object. It is not, however, a quality of the soul! Thus the *Tattva Saṁgraha* states: in short, the mind, which is of the nature of both pleasure etc. and the representation (*ākāra*) of phenomena, is an "object of mundane-experience".[44] The term "mind" is also employed in the following manner: the mind is an object [of mundane experience] on account of its association with the qualities *sattva* etc., like the earth etc. As well, it is said: because it acts as the cause in the ascertainment of objects, the mind functions as an organ, like the sense-organs.

An objection is raised: we hold that the dispositions (*dharma* etc.) are as well qualities of the soul!

This is false, as it is improper to attribute the refinement (*saṁskāraka*) of the soul to these! The refining of karmic activities such as the *jyotiṣṭoma* rite etc. does not arise in the soul since there is no change seen to occur in the refinement of the soul by such activities as farming etc. Rather, the locus wherein actions create such refinements must be unconscious (*jaḍa*); in the issue at hand, it must be the mind. The same thing applies to the refinement of knowledge etc. Due to the force of the refinements of knowledge etc., the distinct appearance of things is seen even when the object does not exist, as in dreaming, remembering and imagining. As a result of the preceding, he says:

(49) The internal and external organs are the immediate instruments whereby mundane-experience is accomplished.

A means for the accomplishment of mundane-experience is necessary since without an "object of mundane experience" there is no mundane-experience.[45]

The collection of internal and external organs acts as the immediate means of mundane-experience, which is of the nature of the cognition of joy, suffering, etc. The *Svāyambhuva Āgama* states: mundane-experience is the [bound] soul's cognition, which is characterized by joy, suffering etc.[46] However, this mundane-experience would not arise without the "objects of mundane-experience" e.g., incense, sandalwood, etc.; thus, there needs to be a means for the bringing about of the prior apprehension of the ascert -ainment of pleasure, etc. He illustrates this with examples:[47]

(50) Just as a ruler employs soldiers for conquering, so the soul employs the mind etc. for cognizing etc.

(51) Just as agency belongs to the ruler when conquering rests in the army, so agency belongs to the soul when cognition etc. rest in the mind etc.

(52) The conquest of the army is not for its own sake, but for the sake of accomplishing the things that are desired of the conquest [by the king]; in like manner, this applies to the mind etc. *(buddhādi)*.

(53) Cognition etc., which belong to the mind etc., do not indeed function for their own sake.

Since the organs are insentient, their activities cannot be for their own sake; rather, they serve a purpose for the conscious soul – this is the meaning.

(53B) Thus, the mind and so forth act as the means whereby the activities of cognition and so forth are accomplished.

He now distinguishes the "object of mundane-experience":

(54) The "manifested condition" *(ākāra)* of delusion, suffering, and pleasure is designated by the term "form" [*"rūpa"* qua *"bhāva"*]; what arises from this is bipartite: mental cognition (boddha) and that which is separate from this, i.e., "the object of mundane-enjoyment", *māyā* etc., which is for purpose of that [i.e.; mundane experience].

Since delusion (moha)etc. are *guṇas* that have become manifest, the "constitution" of delusion etc. is designated by the term "form" (*rūpa*) and is the collection of disposition merit etc. and the collection of conceptions, accomplishment etc. (of which the dispositions are causes). Dispositions are twofold. On the one hand, dispositions constitute mental cognition as it belongs to the soul. On the other hand, dispositions act as the "object-of-mundane-experience" as it is exceedingly separated [from the soul] and is constituted by *māyā* etc., the stuff of the worlds etc. Dispositions function as "the object of mundane-experience" because they are the locus of mundane-experience, i.e., because they exist for the purpose of bringing about mundane-experience (in the sense of being connected to mundane-experience).

What is this thing called "form"? He says:

(55) There is the collection of the threefold demerit etc., attachment and the fourfold merit etc.; as *tamas, rajas,* and *sattva,* they arise in the mind as this "form" on account of *karma.*

The "forms" designated as demerit, ignorance and powerlessness are derived from *tamas.* The form designated as attachment is derived from *rajas.* The forms designated as merit, understanding, non-attachment and powerfulness are derived from *sattva.* Due to *karma,* this eightfold form arises as a condition in the mind because of the *guṇas,* the material causes. The *Svāyambhuva Āgama* and other texts state: the *tattvas,* worlds, bodies and so forth arise both immediately on account of *māyā,* the material cause, as well as mediately, on account of *karma,* an auxiliary cause.

Furthermore:

(56) "Release" entails both a complete separation [from such dispositional qualities as dharma and so forth] and an omnipresent condition [of the soul]. However, the cognition of a cloth and so forth entails a limited condition. Therefore, neither qualities [limiting the soul] nor the lack of such qualities can be [directly] attributed to the soul.

Others also hold that "release" entails the complete separation from [the disposition] "merit" and so forth. The revealed writings indeed claim that the conscious and active soul is innately eternal and omnipresent. However, the cognitive dispositions such as the cognition of a cloth and so forth are nonpervasive, i.e., limited. Therefore, the [cognitive] qualities such as demerit etc., which are non-eternal and unlimited, cannot belong to the soul, which is eternal and unlimited.[48] If such qualities are claimed to be in a relation of inherence (*samavāya*) with the soul, the soul would falsely be described as mutable (*pariṇāmitva*). Demerit etc. give rise to three distinctions of the [*sakala*] soul: the *sāṃsiddhika* (natural), *vainayika* (cultivated) and *prākṛta* (worldly). The *Mṛgendra Āgama* says: the *sāṃsiddhikas, vainayikas* and *prākṛtas* [are the designations of the different configurations of dispositional qualities which] belong to the soul. The *sāṃsiddhika* is the quality belonging to the souls that are illuminated by the *saṃskāras* of special virtue. The *sāṃsiddhika* quality is manifested even after the loss of the physical body, as it has been manifested before [the loss of the body]. The *vainayika* is the quality that is manifested by means of worldly experience, reflection, a religious preceptor and the revealed writings. The *vainayika* quality is purified by the activities of the body, mind and speech.

The *prākṛta* is the quality that is manifested only in the association with a physical body, like the cognition during the dream state.[49]

Thus, being of these three varieties, merit etc. are now described in terms of the differences in their results:

> (57) In order,[50] the results of these are: life in hell *(adhogati)*, bondage *(bandha)*, impediments *(vighāta)*, and worldly life *(saṃsṛti)*; heaven *(svarga)*, release *(mukti)*, absorption in prakṛti *(prakṛtibhāva)*, and non-impediments *(avighāta)*.

> (58-59) Sāṃsārika existence *(bhāva)*, disgrace, obstacles, inability to overcome mundane-experience, the attendance over those of a lower station, possession of a correct insight, absence of the desire for mundane-experience, and the obstacle to what one proposes to accomplish–these are the results of the *sāṃsiddhika* dispositions; the *vainayika* and *prākṛta* dispositions belong to those mentioned [in v.57].[51]

"Life in Hell" etc. are the results that come to be, in order, from demerit etc., i.e., from the *vainayikas* and *prākṛtas*. "Wordly life" etc. are a result of the *sāṃsiddhika*. "Life in hell" means the attainment of hell. "Bondage" is not in the soul but in the ego's self-conceit. "Worldly life" is the birth in the womb of animals etc.[52] "Release" is the release according to other systems, since according to the *Mokṣa Kārikā* the highest form of release can only arise on account of *dīkṣā*. "Absorption into *prakṛti*" is a union (*laya*) with *prakṛti*.

"Worldliness" refers to *saṃsāra*. "Disgrace" refers to the degradation of one's condition. The "non-overcoming of mundane-experience" is the passion for mundane-experience. The "attendance over beings of a lower station" is the superintendence over those who are of a lower station than oneself; "possession of a correct insight [concerning one's higher station]" is the correct understanding of the respective objects [of one's station]". The rest is clear. Having discussed the dispositions, he now treats the conceptions (*pratyaya*).

(60) As the awakened cognition (*saṃbuddhi*) of the manifest, unmanifest, and the soul, attainment (*siddhi*) thus arises on account of the collection of *dharma* and so forth. This collection is slightly connected to *rāga* [i.e., *vairāgya*]

In our system, the eight dispositions–merit etc.–subsist in the mind (*buddhi*) in a latent form (*vāsanātva*). Thus, it is said: the dispositions (*bhāvās*) are so called because they cause the subtle body (*liṅga*) to arise (*bhāvayanti*).[53] Furthermore, when the dispositions have reached a developed state and have entered into the condition of being "objects of mundane-experience" in a gross form, they are called "conceptions" on account of causing the mental activity of the bound souls.[54] Thus it is said: the conceptions (*pratyayās*) are so-called because they cause the soul's mental activity (*pratyāyanti*).

Accomplishment arises from the group of four dispositions–merit etc.–which are derived from *sattva* and which are slightly associated with *rajas* in the form of non-attachment (*vairāgya*). *Siddhi* is the attainment of a superior state which is just a cognition of its respective object; this cognition is an "awakened understanding" (*saṃbuddhi*) of the manifested condition of the *guṇas,* the unmanifested condition of *prakṛti* and of the souls. "Accomplishment" is the cognition (*buddhi*) whose object (*viṣaya*) is the soul, *prakṛti* etc.[55] In this case, the soul, which is exceedingly separated, shines forth independently as the illuminating agent in the cognition of the mind whose object is the manifest and unmanifest. Thus, they describe this as "when the seer abides in his own natural condition."[56] This does not take place on account of the illuminating agency of the mind; such a view would entail the fault of describing the soul as an "object of mundane-experience"; the *Mokṣa Kārikā* states: if the soul is considered to come within the scope of an "object of mundane-experience", the soul becomes subject to mutability.[57]

(61) Mixed with the disposition of demerit etc., contentment *(tuṣṭi)* arises from the threefold collection such as merit etc.; by means of this contentment a satisfying discernment arises when one poorly grasps the soul.

Contentment arises from the threefold, *tamas*-based collection of demerit etc.; this collection is slightly blended with merit etc., which are of a sattvic origin. Contentment occurs through the instrumentality of the attainment that is of the nature of the cognition of the already discussed gross and subtle elements wherein one grasps the nature of the soul according to the various [other] systems.

Contentment is described as a cognition that arises when one, even though unaccomplished, says: "I am [satisfactorily] accomplished." This is due to a non-attachment (*vairāgya*) that is of a lower order. Thus, it is said that contentment is the cognition of the [soteriologically] unaccomplished soul that: "I am accomplished."[58]

(62) Incapacity arises on account of the threefold collection of demerit etc., coloured by a little *rāga;* incapacity is the lack of effectiveness in attaining prosperity etc.

"Prosperity" (*śubha*) here refers to "the activity of the organs of generation" described as joy. The "lack of effectiveness" in "prosperity etc." stems from a defect in the organs or, by implication, the body. This "incapacity" originates out of the tāmasika group, which is slightly connected to *rajas.* It is said that incapacity arises on account of inactivity. Since incapacity is of the nature of suffering,it is of a tāmasika origin; it is also of a rājasika origin, as the [rājasika] quality (which is in association with the cause), is seen in the effect.[59]

(63) Error is the discernment of an object otherwise than it is. Error arises devoid of a connection to *rāga,* although error is slightly connected to merit etc.

"Error" arises on account of the tāmasika group, which is devoid of *rajas* and which is slightly connected to *sattva.* Error is the grasping of an object as otherwise than it is, and is characterized by delusion (*moha*), extreme delusion, mental darkness and extreme mental darkness (*andhatāmisra*). It is said that error is the perception of one thing as another, for the reason that the two [confused] things share a particular common element.

Having briefly discussed the dispositions and conceptions, he concludes the topic of mental cognition (*buddhi-bodha*):

> (64Aa) Briefly stated, this [collection of dispositions and conceptions] is a quality of the mind *(buddhi).*

The *Mataṅga Āgama* and other texts provide a detailed account of the dispositions and conceptions. In the *Mṛgendra Vṛtti Dīpikā* these have also been elucidated and accurately determined by us. From a fear of dealing with too many minute details, I am not delineating any further details here.

> (64Ab) This *[buddhi-dharma]* is experienced by consciousness [i.e., the soul].

"Since it is an object of mundane-experience" should be supplied [in v. 64Ab].

He now establishes the condition of being an "object of mundane-experience":

> (64b-65a) When an "object of mundane-experience" arises, whatever arises is apprehended; this apprehension *(anubhava)* is "mundane-experience" and is sufficient for explaining the "mundane-experiencer" *(bhoktṛ).*

The "object of mundane-experience" is characterized by the transitory cognitive activities originating in the mind. These transitory cognitions cannot be attributed to the mundane-experiencer, since this experiencer's mode of consciousness is nontransitory and eternally of an apprehending nature (*grāhaka*).

(65B) Without the one who accomplishes *(sādhayitṛ)*, [the postulation of] "desire" cannot be logically explained.

This verse is directed against the Buddhists who hold that "the mind is itself consciousness" (*buddi-caitanya-vāda*). By appealing to a conception of an impermanent mundane-experiencer of *buddhi*-based cognition, the Buddhists hold the view that the "mind is itself consciousness" for the following reasons: (1) the insentiency (like a pot etc.) [of the impermanent mundane-experiencer]; (2) the impossibility of the mundane-experiencer being the result of karmic action from another time and (3) the condition of being an "object of mundane-experience", like what is spoken.

The verse postulates that the activity of mundane-experience (*bhoga-kriyā*) cannot be logically explained without the postulation of an active mundane-experiencer; as well, on account of the activity of mundane-experience, the soul is established as the agent involved in that activity. In the verse "desire" is "want".

An objection is now raised:

(66A) Without the concurrence (*saṃvāda*) with something perceptible (*dṛṣṭa*) there can be no proof of an inference.

According to the above position an inference must be seen to have a concurrence with another means of proof (*pramāṇa*) [i.e., *pratyakṣa*]; for example, fire is inferred from smoke once one has actually been present and directly perceived [the concomitance of smoke and fire]. The validity of an inference can only be established in this manner.

The Buddhists claim that one cannot establish a "self" that is the mundane-experiencer and separated from cognition, due to the absence of any means of proof [applicable in this case], as there is indeed the doubt raised by the fallacy of the unsupportable conclusion (*vyabhicāra*) concerning the inference regarding the mundane-experiencer: "experience" itself allows of no apprehension of a constitutive distinction (*ākāra-bheda*) between a "cognizer" and "cognition", as we only discern cognition as "apprehension" (*anubhava*). No such fallacy of the unsupportable conclusion (*vyabhicāra*) exists concerning the thing inferred (*sādhya*) in such examples as the smoke on the mountain top. They say: this consciousness is of a single nature capable of modification into manifold forms, such as joy, depression, etc. In this case you can use any "term" you so desire [to describe one of the manifold 'modifications'].

This is false! He says:

(66B) For whatever reason that there is this concurrence with something perceptible, for that reason there is the validation of this concurrence.

The meaning of the verse is as follows. It is not proper to hold that, on account of the existence of a "conflict with activity" (*kriyā-virodha*) arising when one attributes inpermanent cognition to the soul, a false attribution of permanency [in one's soul] takes place. It is said: having an apprehending nature, the soul is established on the basis of the apperception (*saṃvedana-pratyakṣa*) due to a condition of permanency established on account of the "manifestation" that appears by means of a condition of permanency in the form of an "object" (*viṣayatva*) that is only sensed within the body as in sleep etc., wherein there is no proximity to external objects; this apprehension (*anubhava*) is the awareness (*saṃvedana*) of an object and is [classified as] mundane-experience.[60]

This is also said [by the Buddhists]: all things are momentary on account of the "conflict with activity" resulting when both sequentiality and simultaneity are attributed to that which is non-momentary.

This is false due to the example of the gem, a permanent thing: at one and the same time various objects such as pots etc. can appear sequentially reflected in the one gem.

Furthermore, since whatever is momentary is destroyed the moment it arises, it is impossible for there to be a "conformity with the activity" with manifold instants that no longer exist.

In the commentary on the *Mataṅga Āgama* and elsewhere such arguments are carried out in detail by the Ācārya [Rāmakaṇṭha II].

Thus, holding that the soul can be inferred by means of the establishment of self-consciousness (*svasaṁvedana*), he says:

> (67A) Herein there is no concurrence with a means of valid knowledge *(pramāṇa)* since the means of valid knowledge is perception.

In this case there is no need for there to be a concurrence with another *pramāṇa* of this *pramāṇa* [i.e., *pratyakṣa*].

Although "perception" lacks a concurrence with another *pramāṇa,* validity (*prāmāṇya*) is the result of the cognition of an unapprehended object (*anadhigata-viṣaya*); the Buddhists say: a *pramāṇa* is the comportment towards an unapprehended object (*anadhigata-artha-gantṛ-pramāṇam*).

Again, how does the fallacy of the unsupportable conclusion apply in the case of the mountain top, etc. He says:

> (67B) The fallacy of the unsupportable conclusion is refuted by the positive and negative instances [of the inference].

The fallacy of the unsupportable conclusion does not apply in the example of smoke etc. In this case, the connection *(saṃbandha)* is an inseparable concomitance *(avinābhāva)* discerned with positive and negative instances. Such is the case with the smoke that has been well discerned to have its locus in fire. However, an error occurs when one does not discern the proper nature of "smokiness" and attributes its genesis to the mountain-top itself. Therefore, here as well, on account of discerning the antecedence of the agent *(kartṛ-pūrvakatva-darśana)*of actions in all cases, the mundane-experiencer is inferred from the activity of mundane-experience. By you as well, the mind in another's body is inferred by an inference without the concurrence with another *pramāṇa,* because of the activity of the effect [i.e., the body], which is established by the prior existence of the mind in one's own body. Thus, he says:

(68A) The mind is established as the cause in the explanation regarding the characteristics *(dharma)* of the body;

This is the meaning. The cause that explains one's bodily characteristics, i.e., movement and so forth, also explains the cause of such characteristics in another's body–i.e., the mind. Concerning this the Buddhists say: having seen, in one's own body, the activity that is preceded by the mental activity, on account of seeing it elsewhere [i.e., in another's body], the mind is recognized [as preceding the activity]. Therefore, the mundane-experiencer is established by the presumption of mundane-experience (*bhoga-anyathā-anupapatti*)[61], like the sense of sight etc. [which is inferred] by means of the presumption from the discernment of colour etc. He says:

(68B-69Aa) The *pramāṇa* of that which is other than that which is generally accepted as perceptible is established by means of inference.

Cārvāka says: let there be a mundane-experiencer, but that too is just the body which is of the nature of a manifestation of a modified aggregate of the elements such as earth etc. As the manifestation of the ability to intoxify arises as a result of a fermenting agent (*kiṇva*), etc., so the appearance of consciousness arises as a modified characteristic of the body. Furthermore, since the activity of mundane-experience etc. appears to exist on account of the power of the vital forces such as *prāṇa,* nothing else but perception can be appealed to [in order to account for the manifestation of consciousness]. Thus, they say: it is impossible to postulate something imperceptible when something perceptible [already] exists.

He rejects this view:

(69A.b-70A) As the [physical] cause [of consciousness], let the aggregate of the earth and so forth account for consciousness qua the mundane-experiencer of the cognitive activity of the mind. This is wrong!

Consciousness is not like a pot and so forth; proof of this is based on the observation concerning the sphere of the objects of mundane-experience: hard touches, soft touches, and so forth on the outside of the body are felt as pain, pleasure, and so forth within the body. Therefore, it follows that the soul is established by means of being the mundane-experiencer even in the case of the body; furthermore, there is no means of proof to establish that consciousness belongs to the body. He says:

(70B) Indeed, how can you come up with a decisive proof to establish that consciousness belongs to the body?

There is the objection [by Cārvāka]: Consciousness is just of the nature of the body, as it is only observed when there is the existence of the elements that give rise to the body (which is of the nature of sperm and blood) and it is not observed when the body is non-existent.

(71A.a) Even when there is the existence [of the body], the fallacy of over-generality (*anaikāntika*) applies;

In the case of the existence of the elements constituting the foetus etc., or a corpse, consciousness is not observed; therefore, consciousness is not of the nature of the body. Thus it is said that there is no proof to substantiate the claim that the soul is the body. He says:

(71A.b) Consequently, "the cawing of crows" [i.e., such is the sense of your argument].

Since it is an "object of mundane-experience", consciousness is not of the nature of the body; he says:

(71B-72A) Such things as molasses and so forth are "objects of mundane-experience", perceptible and incapable of manifesting consciousness. The body is equal to molasses and so forth, as it is an "object of mundane-experience" as an "image" (*chāyā*) belonging to the soul.

Molasses and such things are made objects of experience (*viṣayī-kriyamāṇa*) as objects that are "grasped", i.e., "mundanely experienced", through a cognitive experience of the nature of an "image" (*chāyā*) belonging to the soul. Such objects as molasses etc. are never observed to be manifested forms of consciousness (*abhivyakta-cetana*). Therefore, with reference to the position already stated that the soul is the body qua an aggregate of elements, the non-consciousness of the body is due to the process whereby something is made "an object of experience" as an object of mundane-experience, i.e., as something which is "grasped"; thus, the mundane-experience cannot be established to belong to the body. Moreover, if consciousness is indeed said to belong to the body, it would be impossible for an older person to remember something from childhood due to the repeated changes in the body which lead to the destruction of previous states! Such criticisms [as raised above] are taken up by us in detail in the *Mṛgendra Āgama Vṛtti Dīpikā*.

A new objection is raised by those who claim that the senses are consciousness: let the mundane-experiencer be identified with the senses, which are separate from the body. That this is false, he says:

(72B-73A) As the organs (*karaṇa*) for [the presentation of] "the objects of mundane-experience", the senses cannot be identified with consciousness; therefore, having consciousness intrinsic to it, the soul is the mundane-experiencer.

As previously stated, the senses are for the purpose of bringing about mundane-experience. Since they are "objects of mundane experience" and organs [lit., "instruments" (*karaṇatva*)], like swords etc., the senses most certainly cannot be [identified with] consciousness. Agency (*kartṛtva*) cannot belong to the sense-organs but belongs to the soul, which has consciousness as constitutive of its nature, since the agency of the soul accounts for the "engagements in" and "cessations of" all other agentive activities that are caused by an agent. They say: "the Lord is the one responsible for engagements in and cessations of agentive activities. The Lord is the 'Unengaged one'; the one who is responsible for the causative process (*kāraka*) is the agent (*kartṛ*)."

(73B) The mundane-experience of the mundane-experiencer is the manifestation of consciousness coloured (or impassioned, *anurañjita*) by the image (*chāyā*) of "the objects of mundane experience."

The mundane-experience of the mundane-experiencer is the manifestation of consciousness coloured (*anurañjita*) through the [mental] "presentation" (*ākāra*) which is an image (*chāyā*) of the nature of pleasure etc. that belong to the mind, which is an "object of mundane-experience". The *Svāyambhuva Āgama* states: mundane-experience is the consciousness characterized by the [bound] soul's mundane-experience etc.

A new topic is introduced:

(74A) Consciousness appears as "an object of mundane-experience" on account of the connection of that which is not conscious with that which is conscious.

Even though it is not of the nature of consciousness, the "object of mundane-experience", which is of the nature of the mind, appears as if it is of the nature of consciousness on account of its connection to the consciousness constitutive of the soul.[62] Sāṁkhya says: that which is not conscious appears as if it is conscious.

Moreover:

(74B-75A) Mutually constituted by the connection of the

reflection of the non-conscious and the conscious, souls and bonds appear very strongly [as of one nature] through the instrumentality of mundane-experience.

The "object of mundane-experience" is both a "thing" (*vastu*) superintended over by consciousness (*citta-adhiṣṭhita*) and a collection of the organs of the mind. It presents the "object" to the soul. The soul [in turn] grasps the mental activity of the mind. They say: the soul (*puruṣa*) is cognizant on account of the mental activity of the mind.[63] The "phenomenal connection" (*ākāra-anuṣaṅga*) is just a "contact" (*saṃśleṣa*) of the two "images" (*chāyā*) or "reflections" (*pratibimba*) that are of the nature of the conscious and the unconscious; due to this connection, the souls, mundane-experiencers and bonds are transformed into "objects of mundane-experience" through the form of the "object" (*viṣaya*) that arises through the instrumentality of the mental activity of the mind, which itself functions in a mirroring manner and is called mundane-experience. For this reason, the saṁsārins make the mistake of seeing the soul and so forth in what is not the soul etc. However, through discernment there is the dissolution of *prakṛti* for the saṁsārins. Sāṁkhya defines this dissolution as release. Thus:

> (75B) Mundane-experience [which appears] in the "object of mundane-experience" [i.e., in the mind] is a reflection of the soul, like the moon in water.

Mundane-experience that is characterized as an "object of mundane-experience" solely belongs to the pervasive and lordly soul.

In the cognitive activity of the mind, which is of the nature of ascertainment, there is a reflection, like the reflection of the moon in water; this reflection is characterized by the manifestation of consciousness. However, the example [supporting the metaphor] is only applicable to a "naturally occurring manifestation" as the moon reflection is of a purely insentient and material nature. Therefore, on account of the condition of the mundane-experiencer, agency solely belongs to the conscious soul, and cannot be said to belong to the mind and its products, which are non-conscious and "objects of mundane-experience".[64]

But [objects Sāṁkhya], agency entails engagement in activity;[65] if agency is attributed to the soul, the soul becomes subject to transformation (*pariṇāmitā*). Since the soul is not subject to transformation (*nirvikāra*), agency cannot be attributed to the soul. Rather, agency just belongs to [the sphere of] *prakṛti;* prior to the arising of discriminative knowledge, *prakṛti* shows itself to the *puruṣa* through the instrumentality of the mind and its products, which are '"objects of mundane-experience"—in this manner *saṃsāra* is described. According to Sāṁkhya, release is the ceasing of the activity that arises with this *prakṛti.* Thus, they say: having shown herself to the audience the dancer draws away from the audience; likewise, having manifested itself to the *puruṣa, prakṛti* ceases from its activity.[66] As a result, he says:

> (76A-78B) When mundane-experience is not attributed to the soul out of a fear of attributing transformation [to the soul], then the difficulty arises concerning the identity (aviśeṣa) of the released one and the bound one.[67]

The meaning of the verse is as follows: agency is not the [direct] engagement in activity; rather, just the "capacity for activity" (*śaktitva*) is engaged in activity. For instance, like the iron fillings that have come within the proximity of a magnet, the locus of activity (*kriyāveśa*), which is of the nature of movement (*spanda*), solely belongs to the body, which is in proximity to the soul. Therefore, there is no possibility of the transformation of the soul during the [activity of] mundane experience, which is of the nature of the "representational activity" of the mind and its products.

However [objects the Śaivite], this "representational activity" takes place as something separate [from the *puruṣa*].[68] But, when you do not postulate this separate condition in the case of the soul that is without impurity (*nirmalatva*) of the soul, the difficulty arises as to the identity (*aviśeṣa*) of the one who mundanely experiences and the one who is liberated, since both are similarly unconnected [i.e., even the bound soul is not connected to the impurity mundane-experience entails].

No! It is said: *prakṛti* purposely functions for the sake of another.[69] They say: as the non-conscious milk functions for the sake (*nimitta*) of the growth of the calf, so *prakṛti* functions for the sake of the release of the *puruṣa*.[70] Thus he says:

(77A) Moreover, the view that "the activity of the bonds is for the purpose of the soul" is also opposed!

The meaning of the verse is as follows. It is false to hold that the activity of *prakṛti* is for the sake of the *puruṣa*, as *prakṛti* is nonconscious; as in the case of [non-conscious] milk etc., one observes the activity as it is superintended over by the conscious cow etc. Moreover, even if we accept this type of activity [of purely unconscious things], it does not make sense to say that this activity can be for the sake of something unconnected [to anything], since there is the useful appropriation even of air, water, etc.; or, if the activity be said to be for the purpose of that which is unconnected (*nirapekṣa*), then even in the case of the liberated one this activity will occur. Furthermore, on account of the engagement of the bound soul which has a desire for mundane-experience, it is false to attribute mundane-experience to this soul since no change is said to occur in the soul; he says:

(77B) In an unchangeable mundane-experience, as in the case of a liberated soul, mundane-expereince does not arise.

Sāṁkhya objects: non-discrimination (*aviveka*) is the cause of the activity of *prakṛti*. When the discrimination between the *puruṣa* and *prakṛti* exists, "the cessation of the activity" is no longer activity. Therefore, there is no identity (*aviśeṣa*) of the bound one and the released one. They say: it is my belief that there is nothing more beautifully youthful than *prakṛti,* who, with the thought, "I have been seen", does not come within the sight of the *puruṣa* again.[71]

This is false! Given your position, non-discrimination cannot exist, since the soul is pure (*nirmalatva*). And since [according to you] non-discrimination is at all times without a cause, discrimination itself becomes an impossiblity. Therefore, we claim that, by the unestablishment of anything other than non-discrimination, passion (*sarāgata*), impurity (*samalatva*) etc. should be attributed to the soul itself.

If one holds that the innate condition of unconsciousness is roused to consciousness on account of the association with that which is defiled, i.e., with the connection to a body etc., then it follows that the eternal connection to things which are other than what is innate will arise — thus, the opponent's view is put in doubt:

(78A) If it is claimed that, on account of being subject to transformation (*vikāritva*), it is non-eternal (*anitya*).

Here, the "mundane-experiencer" should be supplied in the verse [i.e., if transformation is posited, the mundane-experiencer becomes non-eternal]. He refutes this:

(78Ab) Then the effected condition of *māyā* (*māyāsādhya*) is not recognized.

The "peculiar characteristic" (*viśeṣa*) that is brought about (*kriyamāna*) by means of *māyā* and its effects (*svakaryāni*) through the instrumentality of the subtle and gross bodies is not recognized ("by you" should be supplied here). Therefore, the fault of attributing noneternality and so forth [to the soul] does not apply—this is the meaning [of the verse]. How is this possible? He says:

(78B) And, on account of the intrinsically manifested consciousness, neither transformation nor destruction [can apply to the soul].

Unlike the Naiyāyikas and others, we do not hold that the soul is solely of an unconsciousness nature. Rather, the soul has consciousness innate to its nature.

The Naiyāyikas raise the following question: concerning the innateness of this consciousness [in the soul] since consciousness does not arise without a connection to a body etc., what is the beginningless thing by which the bound condition [of the soul] is discerned [by the Śaivites]?

[The Answer follows:] He is going to say that this [beginningless thing] is just *mala*. And thus, when there is the removal of *mala* by means of *māyā* — i.e., by *kalā* etc., which are its effects — the total manifestation of the innate nature of the soul takes place. When *mala* ripens by means of *Śiva-śakti* — which is designated as *dīkṣā* — all objects become manifested. Thus, he says in the verse, "neither transformation nor change" belongs to the soul. He says of the soul:

> (79A) *Rāga* serves the role of "objectifying" [in the presentation of] the object of mundane-experience. Since *rāga* is like a crystal [i.e., since it simply manifests things], it cannot be the cause as discussed above.

Rāga gives rise to the presentation of the "object of mundane experience", which is manifested in the form of *sukha, duḥkha* and *moha.*

Rāga is said to be "like a crystal" because it manifests things by means of its own luminosity. *Rāga* is not a cause of that "transformation" [of the innate consciousness of the soul] as discussed above. It is said that "the affliction to the attachment to objects" (*viṣayoparāga*) is just "the making something of an object" (*viṣayikaraṇa*) through the intentional-activity towards it.

In spite of the repeated transformation of the body, which is an "object of mundane-experience", no transformation can be attributed to the mundane-experiencer.

> (79B-80A) The soul is not transformed when the body undergoes transformation; attributing transformation to the soul entails describing it as unconscious and as an object of mundane-experience, like the mind.

This is the meaning: If the soul is subject to transformation, unconsciousness and the fact of being an object of mundane-experience apply to it, like the mind etc.

Herein, after having proposed another's viewpoint, he will criticize it:

(80B-81A) Consciousness is rather the "quality" described as a "cognition" that is in a relation of inherence [with the soul]. Therefore, consciousness cannot be shown to be intrinsic to the soul. This is false!

The Naiyāyikas and others argue that the soul is by nature unconscious; on account of the connection of *manas* with the soul, cognition arises as a quality [of the soul]. This cognition is solely the consciousness of the soul; in no other way can the soul be considered to be a conscious nature.

This is false: as in the case of a pot etc., there can be no connection of inherence of cognition to the soul if the soul is considered to be unconscious.

Another objection is raised: herein, the restricting factor [in the relation between cognition and the unconscious soul] is *karma*, designated as "the imperceptible force" (*adṛṣṭa*). Bound cognition arises in a relation of inherence with the soul only when the soul is a common substratum of *karma*. This cognition does not arise in other places, i.e., in different substrata, such as in pots, etc. Thus, he says:

(81B-82A) Consciousness exists in the unconscious soul and nowhere else. But even *karma* is not suitable as the restricting factor, since *karma* is found in a different locus.

It is said that due to the possibility of attributing transformation [to the soul], there is no [soteriological] development (*saṃskāratva*) of the soul but just the [soteriological-] development of *prakṛti*, since this development is like the activity of agriculture etc. Therefore, even *karma* cannot be the restricting factor. Thus, the soul is innately conscious, since it has consciousness as an intrinsic part of its nature. He says:

(82B-83A) According to the wise, in the same way that delusion *(moha)* exists on account of those who have delusion intrinsic to them, and not otherwise, so consciousness exists on account of conscious things, and not otherwise.

According to the opponent, "cognition" is considered to be of the nature of consciousness and is considered to be a "quality" of the soul. However, according to this position, when the quality is destroyed, the destruction of the substratum is also entailed, due to the inseparability of the substratum and quality! Thus, the soul ought to be accepted as always having consciousness intrinsic to it. It is said: since the innately conscious soul is veiled by *mala, manas,* the mind etc. are established as the manifesting agents of limited consciousness.

He is now going to describe *kalā, vidyā* and *rāga,* which are collectively described as "the triadic sheath". In terms of the means whereby mundane-experience arises, these *tattvas* lie above *prakṛti*; they collectively act as an instigating-agent by means of acting as an "auxiliary cause" in the activity of the soul's mundane-experience. He say:

> (83B-84A) The triad, which is designated to be above *prakṛti,* is an organ for the instigation and a cause of the excitation in the "object of mundane-experience"; as well, this triad exists as an agent in the soul's activity of mundane-experience.

Having dealt with mundane-experience in this manner, he is now going to speak about the arising of the ego from the mind, which originates from *prakṛti.*

> (84b-85a) The grouping in the mind which is a posterior division gives birth to the ego. The *guṇas* are considered to be the progenitors. The *guṇas* are also manifested in the imagination etc.

The *guṇas* are manifested as the material-causes of the effect according to the maxim: on account of interaction, interdependency and mutual subjugation. Hence, the [*guṇika*] cause exists in the imagination etc., i.e., in the modifications of the mind. Sāṁkhya claims: the *guṇas* function interrelatedly on account of mutual subjugation and cooperation.[72] Therefore, on the one hand, the mind generates "ascertainment" [and thus gives rise to the imagination etc.] and on the other, the mind generates the ego, which consists of its own particular "blending of the *guṇas*". Thus, according to the maxim that "more than one progenitor is required" the *guṇas* are considered to be the progenitors that are mutually blended together [in the generated effect]. In like manner [i.e., as mutually blended together], the *guṇas* exist in all objects. Thus, when we say that such and such a thing is *sāttvika* etc., we mean that it contains a *guṇika* abundance of *sattva* etc. Just as mud takes on many different forms, as in pots etc., so the *guṇas* are in a direct association with the effect as a result of direct participation.

He says:

(85A-86B) "The first transformation of the *guṇas* takes place by the arising and dominating [of one over the other]" — but this settled condition should remain invariable!

An objection is raised: if the *guṇas* are in an invariable relation whereby they mutually suppress one another, they cannot be the progenitors of [soteriological] "accomplishment" [*siddhi qua buddhi-pratyaya*] etc.; therefore, just let the ego arise from the *guṇas* in a direct association with the *guṇas*. He says:

(86B-87A) O pundits, do not prater that this [same] maxim applies to the ego as well. Because of the generative transformation [of the *guṇas*], even the subtle elements are in association with the *guṇas*.

On account of the serial transformation of the *guṇas* — as it is said, on account of the generative transformation of everything beginning with the ego and ending with the gross elements — this association with the *guṇas* not only applies to the ego but to the subtle elements as well (which means the collection of the organs and the collection of the gross elements). It is, therefore, correct to hold that, as in the case of the association of the shapes of earth in pots, skulls, etc., not all things arise directly from the *guṇas.*

He now addresses the question: what are the *guṇas* and by means of what activities are they effected? He says:

> (87B-88A) *Sattva, rajas* and *tamas*—these are the *guṇas* that are the causes in the mind; with respect to each soul they are manifested by means of the restrictions of the manifested activities.

As stated earlier, the object that is an "object of mundane-experience" for the soul arises through the instrumentality of the mind in the form of the dispositions, conceptions and so forth. The *guṇas* were the cause at the beginning of creation and continue to maintain this creation to the present time; as well, the *guṇas* are the cause of the mind.

Since these *guṇas* are mutually-interconnected, they are categorized as a single *tattva.* Thus, it is said: even though the *guṇas* are three in number, they are still considered to constitute one *tattva* on account of their inseparability.[73] Therefore, the accomplishment of *sattva* etc. occurs by means of the activities referred to as the "restriction of the manifested activities". The activities occur by means of the causality of the mind and are manifested because of the dominance [of one particular quality over the other two].

The *Āgamas* state that there are other effects of the *guṇas* as well: steadiness, patience, etc.; valour, cruelty, etc.; and discontent and slowness.

Sāṁkhya raises an objection: the *guṇas* exist as eternal conditions constitutive of *prakṛti.* That this is false, he says:

> (88B-89A) Since the *guṇas* are both unconscious and manifold, they have a cause, just as does the mind, pots, etc.

Like pots and so forth, the *guṇas* are of an unconscious and manifold nature and are, therefore, "effects".

What is the cause of the *guṇas*? He says:

(89B-90A) The cause of the *guṇas* is *prakṛti;* undivided in *prakṛti,* the *guṇas* begin their activity when Śiva induces *prakṛti.*

The *guṇas* exist as undivided and subtle conditions in *prakṛti;* Śiva induces them to develop into a gross form through the distinctions of their respective activities. The verse states that Śiva induces *prakṛti.* Since *prakṛti* is of an unconscious nature, the *prakṛti*-activity is not self-willed [and therefore depends on the inducement of Śiva]. Furthermore, as each soul is separately linked to *prakṛti* through the engagement in a subtle body, *prakṛti* is manifold. Since *prakṛti* is manifold, it is an "effect" (I will discuss this further in the sequel).

Souls are bound because they are yoked to *mala.* This bound condition occurs through the condition of being a mundane-experiencer for that soul yoked to the five sheaths, *kalā* etc. *Dīkṣā* purifies this condition and according to the *Āgamas* is above the *prakṛti-tattva.* Since the accomplishment of mundane-experience and the attainment of the particular station of existence cannot arise simply on account of the existence of the mundane-experiencer, the soul [qua mundane-experiencer] is qualified by both consciousness and pervasiveness. Having considered this, he is going to establish the existence of the *rāga-tattva,* which was earlier said to be the cause of the craving for mundane-experience.

(90B-91A) The attachment to the "object of mundane-experience" comes into being when the actual apprehension of the "object of mundane-experience" exists. In order for this attachment to come into being, it is necessary to postulate "*rāga*", which causes the craving for mundane-experience itself.

During *saṃsāra,* an "attachment" arises when the soul discerns an "object of mundane-experience". This attachment does not arise without a cause; otherwise, it could even occur during the state of release. Therefore, *rāga* ought to be accepted as the generating factor in the craving for mundane-experience, which brings about the soul's attachment.

He now expresses an opposite opinion:

(91B-92A) Quite rightly *sattva, rajas,* and *tamas* act as the cause-of-the-craving for the objects [of mundane-experience]; however, when this craving has arisen in the mind of the soul, this other thing [i.e., *rāga*] is of no use!

The manifested condition of the object of mundane-experience is solely a result of the three *guṇas* (*sattva* etc.), which arise in the mind in a transformed state as pleasure, suffering and delusion. The "transformed" *guṇas* thus appear in the mind in terms of the ascertained appearance of the object; in turn, this ascertainment serves to bring about mundane-experience, which itself is influenced by the predominance of one of the three *guṇas.* It is, therefore, clear that some cause must be postulated in order to account for the soul's desire for this "object of mundane-experience". Hence, *rāga* ought to be considered to be this cause and should be considered to have its locus in the grasper, the one who apprehends the "object of mundane-experience", which is constituted by the three *guṇas* (*sattva* etc.) and is produced in the mind in the form of the *guṇas,* objects, etc.

He now refutes this opponent:

(92B-93A) If the cause of the mind's desire for the "object of mundane-experience" is considered to be in the mind (*buddhi*) itself, i.e., in the form of a "disposition" (*bhāva*), then something other than this "disposition" must be proven [to be the cause of the craving].

The verse addresses the opponent: if you hold that the cause of the attachment solely belongs to the objects of mundane-experience, then it will be impossible to ever be free from *rāga*! Thus the *Tattva Saṁgraha* states: *rāga* is the desirous attachment that causes the soul's engagement in the "object of mundane-experience"(v. 10); indeed, if *rāga* is considered to be of the character of the "object of mundane-experience", then it could not provide any freedom from *rāga.*

An objection is raised. If *rāga* is postulated as the mental disposition characterized as "bondage", the same fault holds. Thus, he responds that even if *rāga* is considered to be a "disposition" the same fault holds. This is what he means: there is no causative factor involved in the creation of "effects" in the *vāsanā* condition characterized by [the disposition] "bondage". If something in a *vāsanā* state were capable of producing effects, given that the *vāsanās* are infinite in the mind, the soul would be confronted with the simultaneous formation of an infinite number of opposing activities—an unacceptable conclusion.[74]

Even if *rāga* is held to be that which has "entered into" the condition of the "object of mundane-experience" through the gross form of the nature of a "conception" [i.e., *pratyaya*], then the same difficulty already mentioned arises, i.e., to be free from *rāga* becomes impossible. Now [you might claim that] *rāga* ought to be construed as something other than either *rāga* for a mind-based disposition. However, if you claim that *karma* should be the cause of the craving, we disagree, for two reasons.[75] In the first case, there is no way of proving that *karma* is the cause responsible for bringing about effects other than those the individual is responsible for bringing about, as in the case of farming etc. In the second place, if *karma* is postulated as the cause of this craving, a manifold number of activities are therefore postulated.[76]

Now, the *vidyā-tattva* is established:

> (93B-94A) Without an instrument, an agent's ability to act cannot be engaged in any activity; thus, *vidyā* is the instrument that serves in the discrimination of the mind's cognitive activity.

As it has been said, this occurs on account of the proximity of the objects that have been presented by the senses. When an object is grasped–an "activity" described as the cognitive activity of the mind–what then ought to be the instrument whereby the soul's grasping activity takes place? That instrument is *vidyā*.[77]

Here an opponent says:

(95B-95A) Like a light, the mind is the illuminating agent of both itself and other things. A "*vidyā*" construed as the instrument whereby the soul cognizes – of what use is it?

[An objection is raised.] Because of the nature of its illuminating property, which is like a lamp, the mind causes the representation of the object as well as itself to be illuminated. No other instrument can be established!

He refutes this [objection]:

(95B-96A) In the apprehension of objects such as pillars etc., a light acts as the instrument for the soul and in the apprehension of a light, the eye [is the instrument]–the same analogy holds in the case of the mind.

The verse points out that an instrument must be postulated in order to account for the activity whereby the mind becomes an apprehended object. The *Tattva Saṁgraha* states: "like the sun, the mind has a manifesting nature; however, since the mind is an object-of-activity [whereby it is apprehended], the mind requires some other instrument in order for it to be grasped."[78] He points this out:

(96B-97A) Since it is of the nature of the three guṇas, the mind, in its presentative-form as the object, is not capable of illuminating itself through discrimination. On its own, it would remain undiscriminated.

(96B-97A) *Vidyā* is above the sphere of the *guṇas*; as the instrument of discrimination, *vidyā* is separated from the sphere of that which is discriminated. Since *vidyā* is capable of discriminating things for the soul, it requires no further instrument.

Of the nature of the three *guṇas*, the mind is an object of that activity whereby it is discerned in the form of "an object of mundane-experience"; therefore, the mind is not self-illuminating, like a lamp etc. But, as it is beyond the sphere of the mind, *vidyā* is separate from the form of "the object of mundane-experience". In causing the illumination of that which is to be known by the soul, *vidyā* does not require a further instrument.

He now describes the function of *kalā*:

(98B-99A) For the purpose of bringing about mundane-experience, there is an instigator of the multitude of agentive-factors involved in actions etc. The self-willed soul is the agent [qua instigator]; *kalā* is the instigating-factor.

It is said that the soul is the agent since it is the instigating agent of the collection of concomitant agentive factors such as the mind etc., which exist for the purpose of bringing about mundane-experience (which takes place on account of the mundane-experiencer).[79] The one who is the Lord of the concomitant agentive factors involved in both the activity and the cessation of activities, and yet who is neither active nor inactive, is the one who is designated as an agent as well as a concomitant agentive factor. In the authoritative texts *kalā* is called the "instigating-agent" in the activity of mundane-experience, since the causative activity of *kalā* is similar to that of the Lord.

An objection is raised by Sāṁkhya: the soul is not an agent! He says that this is false:

(99B-100A) If one holds that [the soul is] not an agent, the very term mundane-experiencer becomes meaningless [as the mundane-experience of the mundane-experiencer is an activity, mundane-experience entails agency]; as well, the activity of *prakṛti* would not bring about any effects [as the effects of *prakṛti*, such as the mind etc., are "instruments" and require an agent].

Due to the activity of mundane experience [i.e., due to the fact that mundane-experience qua activity entails agency], the agency of the soul is established solely on the basis of the mundane-experiencer. If one claims that the soul is not an agent, the activity of *prakṛti*—which exists for the purpose of mundane-experience—becomes fruitless, because of the uselessness of a connection to instruments etc. in something which is not an agent.

Moreover:

(100B-101A) Since they are a means of activity, the motor organs etc. are in the service of an agent. The agent, spoken of as "covered etc." [by *mala* etc.] ought to be understood as the soul, which is pervasive.

If the soul is held to be nonpervasive because it lacks extension in space (as the sky etc.), it would be impossible for the mundane-experience of one place to also occur at a different time at another place; for example, it would be impossible for a person from the south to mundanely-experience things in Kashmir. Thus, due to the failure of holding any other position, the soul ought to be accepted as pervasive.[80] The *Parākhyā Āgama* and other texts state that the agentive cause is *kalā*, which manifests the agentive-capacity [of the soul]. Thus, the soul bound to *kalā* is the concomitant agent involved in mundane-experience. The agentive-capacity (*kartṛ-śakti*) of this soul that is an agent does not come to affect [all] objects, because this agentive-capacity is veiled by *mala*. (In the sequel we will discuss both the "capacities" of agency and "consciousness", given that "capacity" is a unity of the two.) *Kalā* has the power of *mala*; *kalā* only partially manifests the soul's agentive-capacity. *Kalā* is thus described as the "agentive-cause", "cause" and "agent".

The "limited" soul appears to be indistinguishably linked to *kalā* and is, therefore, described as the "agent-concomitant" *(kartṛ-kāraka)* in the activity of mundane-experience. The limited soul is the agent since it is the mundane-experiencer, while *kalā* is the concomitant-cause since it is the agentive-cause. The *Mṛgendra Āgama* states: O

Brahmans, so these two, standing together as if indistinguishable in the activity of mundane-experience, are called the agent-concomitant.[81]

> (101B-102A) If one holds that the agent does not require further agentive factors in the sphere of the mundane world, the soul will have to be considered to be omnipotent for all eternity as it will never be bound by *kalā*.

> (102B-103A) Since the soul will be omnipotent [at all times], it will also be omniscient [at all times], like God. However, it is improper to hold that, since it is omniscient, the soul is an agent for the purpose of its own suffering.

If one holds that due to the innate purity of the soul, i.e., due to its lack of any connection to *mala*, it does not require a connection to *kalā*, then, as in the case of Śiva, the soul will be considered to be (a) "omnipotent", since it will not have a connection to a body of the nature of "*paśa*", i.e., *kalā* etc. and (b) "omniscient", since it will be unconnected to any instruments of ignorance.[82] Such an independent soul would not be presided over by Śiva. However, it is improper to hold that this independent, undefiled soul can be an agent engaged in those bodily activities etc., which ultimately exist for the purpose of suffering. Thus, "the grace of *kalā*" is necessarily required in order to account for the limited consciousness and activity of those souls possessed by mundane-experience on account of being veiled by *mala*." He says:

> (103B-104A) Since it is in a state of bondage, the soul is not omnipotent, like Śiva etc.; when it is engaged in mundane-experience, the soul qua agent requires the grace of *kalā*.

Having established *kalā*, he will now describe the generation of *vidyā*, *rāga*, and *prakṛti* from *kalā* :

> (104B-105A) There is another grouping that derives from

kalā; this other grouping is known as *vidyā, rāga* and *prakṛti*, which arise in succession in a pair [i.e., *rāga* and *vidyā]* and singly [i.e., *prakṛti].*

Rāga and *vidyā* sequentially arise as a pair. *Prakṛti* arises separately as a separate reality. Thus, the *Raurava Āgama* states: from *kalā*, the two tattvas—*rāga* and *vidyā*—have arisen, and *prakṛti* as well. (v. 2.15).

The *Ācārya* [i.e., Sadyojyoti] has not taken up the *tattvas* designated as *kalā* and *niyati*, which are mentioned in the *Āgamas*, because these two *tattvas* are self-evident in light of the context [of what has so far been discussed], as nothing would transpire without both the temporal-sequentiality and experiential-restrictiveness of mundane-experience, which is a result of karmic activities.[83] In the case of farming etc., thieves are seen to steal the fruits of [others'] activities when there are no restrictions established by a ruler. "Restriction" (*niyati*) is established as the restricting-principle that accounts for the restriction of the fruits of karmic-activities (such as the *jyotiṣṭoma* sacrifice etc.) to individual mundane-experiencers.

However, it is false to claim that *karma* is itself the restricting principle, for, as it is said, *karma* only generates the fruits of activities. In over-seeing the sphere of mundane-experience, even the Lord's capacity (*śakti*) requires an auxiliary casual factor, which occurs through the intervention of other *tattvas*. Otherwise, none of the *tattvas* would exist.

Time *(kalā)* is established as the factor that separates off various states of the "object of mundane-experience" etc. For example, in statements such as, "He has been enjoying it for a long time," the conceptions of "long", "quickly", etc. are indicative of the "separating" function of time.

It is impossible for time to be eternal, as the Naiyāyikas and others think, because time is of an unconscious and manifold nature, since it takes the form of living beings etc.. The *Mṛgendra Āgama* states: time, which arises from *māyā*, is based on the conception of an "instant" etc.[84]

He will now discuss the collection of *tattvas* constitutive of the subtle body as well as the fact that the subtle body is restricted to each soul separately:

(105B-106A) The tattvas beginning with earth and ending with *kalā* constitute the tattvic collection that leads to the accomplishment of mundane-experience; according to the learned, this collection is restricted to each mundane-experiencer [separately].

Thus, the *Tattva Saṁgraha* states: this group of characteristics, beginning with earth and ending with *kalā*, is bound to each soul.[85] Thus, it is said that this bound soul, under the control of *karma*, is caused to wander in all the bodies born in their respective worlds.

In the event of a single, universal subtle body, there would be no diversity in mundane-experience. However, the diversity of mundane-experience is seen by all to be diverse! He says:

(106B) Otherwise, it is not proper, due to the diversity that is [phenomenally] seen in pleasure etc.

An objection is now raised: in the case of a universal subtle body, the diversity among the fruits of mundane-experience will arise solely on account of the karmic diversities relating to the subtle body.

This objection is false! He says:

(107A) On account of the karmic-diversity, the diversity [of mundane-experience with respect to each mundane-experiencer] is established.

The diversity of mundane-experience is established solely on account of karmic-diversity. "When there is the establishment of the diversity of mundane-experience, the karmic-diversity is inferred"—such logic entails "the fault of the mutual locus". This is the sense of the verse.

Another objection is raised: "The karmic-diversity is

established solely on account of the agentive-diversity, and the diversity of mundane-experience on account of the karmic-diversity. There is no fault of the mutual locus here." He states:

> (107B-108A) Given that the agents of actions are active because of the simultaneous connection to that [i.e., the single collection of *tattvas* constituting the subtle body], how can there be separate actions postulated on account of the separateness of the agents.

There can be no connection between the agent and the action without a connection between the souls covered by *mala* and the subtle bodies etc., which are constituted by *kalā* etc. However, if by means of the simultaneous connection to all the agents, the action is an activity that is in the form of the subtle body, which is a single tattvic collection, how can the distinctions between the various activities come about? This cannot be the case! This is the meaning [of the verse].

An objection is raised: the diversity of the subtle bodies can only be based on the diversity of each soul's "desire"!

We oppose this objection, since the "desire" only arises on account of each soul's connection to a subtle body! And it is false to hold that the diversity of desire arises on account of a single subtle body. Since the phenomenon of the diversity of mundane-experience cannot be explained in any other manner, one is forced to accept the diversity of subtle bodies with respect to each soul.

An opponent may raise the objection that the diversity of subtle bodies is only applicable in the case of the diversity of souls. The Vedāntins uphold that the soul is single. He says:

> (108B) Thus, it follows that the manifoldness applies as well to souls.

If you hold the doctrine that posits just one universal soul, it is impossible to account for the diversity of pleasure, suffering, etc. and the differences of birth, death, etc. Thus, the manifoldness of souls is established because of the diversity of mundane-experience. The refutation of Advaita is taken up by us in the *Mṛgendra Āgama Vṛtti Dīpikā* in detail.

A question is raised: this tattvic-collection that is of the nature of the subtle body, is it pervasive, like the soul, or is it non-pervasive? Thus, he says:

> (109A) The non-pervasiveness of this [tattvic-collection] is established on account of the impossibility of simultaneous functions.

The subtle body manifests [the soul's limited] consciousness and agency. This [manifesting] "activity" of the subtle body certainly does not occur at all places at all times; therefore, the subtle body is not pervasive.

A further objection is raised: if you postulate that the "effects" of the subtle body's activities come about on account of *karma*, which is an auxiliary cause, then a pervasive subtle body can still account for the [limited] manifestation of the soul's consciousness. Hence, as this argument proves, the pervasiveness of the subtle body does not entail the simultaneous genesis of effects in all places! The reply: even this reasoning is false because the subtle body is both a noneternal thing and an "effect" [of some cause], like pots etc. The following verse addresses these objections:

> (109B-110A) It is not proper to claim that the instrumentality of the subtle body is restricted by *karma*; on account of the impossibility of limitless activities, there is no universal pervasiveness [of the subtle body]

A further question is raised. Is the partial manifestation of consciousness due to the nonpervasive nature of the subtle body or of the soul? He says:

> (110B-111A) According to *śruti* there is a problem in holding that the soul is a substratum characterized by transformation etc. During the time that there is the [limited] manifestation of consciousness, which is simultaneous with the nonpervasive [subtle body], the soul remains pervasive.

It is said that if the soul is [considered] non-pervasive, then it would be impossible to have different mundane-experiences in different places. Moreover, in the state of release the necessity of the soul's pervasiveness ought to be acknowledged, since the *Āgamas* claim that the soul has omnipotence and omniscience, like *Śiva.* If one holds that in the state of release the soul is pervasive and in the state of bondage non-pervasive, one must also claim that the soul is unconscious, mutable and so forth; such a position certainly contradicts the authoritative texts' claim that the soul is eternal, pervasive, etc. Thus, the *Mṛgendra Āgama* states: consciousness, which is of the nature of cognition and activity, is intrinsic to souls at all times and in all ways (V.2.5); therefore, in release the soul is pervasive (V.6.7). The qualities of nonpervasiveness, instantaneousness, universality, unconsciousness and so forth do not apply to the soul.

Now, having discussed the creation of the *tattvas* that are individually restricted to each soul through the instrumentality of the subtle body, he is going to speak about the *tattvas* that are "common" to souls, i.e., the *tattvas* that constitute the various "worlds".

(111B) In a different grouping of *tattvas* [than those which constitute the subtle body] there are the groups that constitute the spheres of mundane-experience for the mundane-experiencers.

This is the meaning: the various spheres of mundane-experience of the bound souls relate to the various mundane experiences of the *tattvas* constituting the various worlds etc.; these tattvas are other than the mundane experience relating to the subtle body. He says:

(112A) Having entered into a body born with a world, this tattvic-collection brings about the [respective karmic] results in these souls' respective spheres of mundane-experience.

When the tattvic-collection has entered into the bodies born of their respective worlds on account of the force of *karma,* i.e., when the tattvic collection has entered into the sphere of mundane-experience for the purpose of the activities, this [tattvic-collection] proportionally allows the manifestation of the limited consciousness and activity of the soul. The *Tattva Saṁgraha* states: on account of the force of *karma,* one wanders in all the bodies born with their respective worlds (V.25). As well, the *Mṛgendra Āgama* states: this subtle body, which belongs to the creature, is briefly described as "conscious" (*cit*), because it is born from the contact with consciousness and is an evolute in the womb of *māyā.* Judging that this is not sufficient, I am going to describe the collection of "cosmic" *tattvas* constituting worlds that produce the bases, bodies and objects [of these worlds] (V. 12.34). He is now going to briefly describe the creation of the various worlds.

> (112B-113A) The courses of the gross worlds beginning with hell and ending with truth are superintended over during their generation, subsistence and destruction by *Deśika, Hāṭaka,* and *Kāla.*

Here Kāla is Kālāgni. Hāṭaka is the Pātālādhipati. Deśika is the Lokācārya since he teaches in all the Śāstras; he resides in a place that is above the Satyaloka, and is even above the Viṣṇuloka. The Ananta Śrīkaṇṭha is present in the Rudraloka since in these gross regions he has superintendence in Brahmāṇḍa. Thus:

> (113B–114Ba) The leader of the one hundred Rudras, together with the eight along with the five, reside in the causes of the earlier mentioned elements—not the [gross] elements [born] of the subtle elements, but as the subtle elements [themselves] which are categories of the internal organ.

Vīrabhadra is governor of the Śatarudras, who are the bearers in the Brahmāṇḍa; Vīrabhadra is located in the subtle *pṛthivī-tattva,* which is not to be confused with the gross *pṛthivī.* Likewise in the group of four subtle elements (the subtle water etc.), which is the group of the causative elements (the gross water etc.) together with the collection beginning with the subtle elements and ending with the ego exist in this sphere with those called Sthānu, Guhya, Atiguhya, Guhyatara and Pavitrā; thus, there are the five and eight that are in these worlds. Thus, the *Nandikeśvara Kārikā* states: Brahmā is located in the gross things for the purpose of the objects of mundane-experience of the bodies that are the support of the subtle elements etc. The Rudraśata is of the Kṣetrabhūva and the forty subtle elements. The subtle elements, *manas,* the ego, mind, organs, the best of the yogins, Vāma, etc, are at the summit of the *guṇas* and rule in the *prakṛti-tattva;* the Maṇḍalins have their sphere in *kalā;* he says:

> (114Bb-116B) The eight wise ones, Paiśāca, etc., who take office in the *guṇa*-tattva ought to be worshipped in the mind; in due order the series of stations of Vāma etc. are completely absorbed in the *prakṛti* that is a modification when [dwelling] at the head of the *guṇa*-tattva, which station of existence is pure and of the character of the *guṇas* yet unaccomplished. The collection of regions of the Krodheśvararudras belongs to the *prakṛti* region.

The thirty Rudras, Vāma etc., together with the eight Krodheśvaras, by means of being the Lords of the *prakṛti* sphere, are located at the head of the worlds of the *guṇa* level. On account of the subtle nature of *prakṛti,* it is improper for these Lords to support the worlds—so say the ones who know the Āgamas.

> P(117A) The Maṇḍalas, the eight desirable ones, are in the *kalā-tattva.*

The Maṇḍalas are in the eight worlds in an eight-fold sequentiality of the *kalā-tattva* in association with *rāga* and *vidyā.* Thus, the *Mṛgendra Āgama* states: the *Maṇḍalādhipas* are in the sixty-four groups of the Great Cities that occupy *kalā*, which is the womb of *raga* and *vidyā* (V. 13.152).

Therein it is said that *kāla* and *niyati* have two worlds; restraint is in *niyati* while the capacity to cause things is in *kāla*. Since the worldly states are well treated in the manuals dealing with ritual and elsewhere, they are not going to be treated in great detail here. In these ritual manuals and elsewhere there may be some differences concerning the enumeration of subordinate worlds; however, some of the enumerations are included elsewhere— so there is no inconsistency.

Having discussed the creation of the *tattvas* of the nature of the worlds, he is going to establish *māyā* (qua *kalā* etc.) as the higher material cause of the worlds that have already been discussed:

> (117B-118A) Mahāmāyā is of an unconscious nature and acts as the prime matter in the creation of the manifested world; it also contains within itself the power to create the manifested world.

"Māyā" is "the extensive one" on account of its self-effected pervasiveness in the form of a manifold "flowing". *Māyā* is the latent conception during the "cosmic rest" *(pralaya)* of the whole impure world.

This *māyā* is the seed of the world that is in the form of *kalā* etc. Since it is the prime matter of the worlds and the principle of the manifoldness regarding the worldly differences with respect to each bound soul, *māyā* is both the direct and indirect material cause of everything that is of the form of an effect.

Māyā has the power to create the manifested worlds, i.e., it has self-emanating "powers" that are of a subtle form. In accordance with the ontological doctrine that the effect pre-exists in the cause, i.e., according to the *Satkāryavāda*, *māyā* is simply the intrinsic "power" *(śakti)* latent in all effects; since it is a purely material cause, *māyā* is unconscious, like earth and so forth. In short, *māyā* is the origin of the means whereby mundane-experience is brought about in the sphere of *kalā* and so forth.

He is now going to describe the nature of *māyā* as a collection of inherent powers:

(118-119A) This *mahāmāyā* possesses intrinsic powers; the plurality and manifoldness of the powers is established on the basis of the manifold and endless "effects".

Due to the fact that we observe a manifold variety and innumerable number of "effects" come into being, *māyā* is most certainly constituted by a manifold variety and innumerable number of intrinsic "powers".

An objection is raised. If one holds that *māyā's* manifold variety of inherent "powers" cause manifold effects, and yet, if one also holds that all the forms of capacity are actually inherent capacities of *māyā* itself, then it is unnecessary to postulate further inherent capacities [in the form of the manifold effects] stemming from this inherent power [of *māyā*]. As a result, *māyā* should be considered to be eternal since it is the prime cause; otherwise, an infinite regress [of causes] will follow. This is the sense of the following verse:

(119B-120A) [An objection is raised.] On account of the manifoldness of the non-conscious things, *mahāmāyā* is noneternal! [The reply:] Not being itself manifold on account of its continued existence, *māyā* is eternal, even though it is of an unconscious nature.

Moreover:

(120B-121A) On account of the infinite number of souls, *māyā* must be pervasive; for the purpose of providing mundane-experience, *māyā* causes all effects through all the courses [of things] and through all the abodes.

Bṛhaspati says: [if *māyā* is not eternal,] all the Siddhas' words, which have been vocalized over a long period of time, will perish.

Although *māyā* is eternal, the various courses [of things

caused by *māyā*] are not infinite. The maxim that "curd comes from milk" supports the idea that transformation is not a total transformation; the maxim that "insects [taking sustenance] from the ghee" also supports the idea that transformation is only partial.

(121B-122A) Creation, maintenance, and destruction are said to be the conditions inherent in *māyā*; the transformation of these inherent conditions begins with the *tattvas* and ends with the worlds.

Since it is the ultimate material cause, *māyā* is responsible for the creation, maintenance and destruction of the universe. The transformation of the worlds, etc. remains as an inherent condition of *māyā* in the form of *tattvas*, etc. Indeed, the universe, as a transformation of *māyā*, consists of the *tattvas*, material things, sentient beings and worlds.

An objection: the *Āgamas* claim that *bindu* is the material cause of the pure *tattvas* etc.

True! That holds good in the case of the higher condition of release, such as is obtained by the Vidyeśvaras etc., but not here, however, as the material cause (qua *māyā*) provides the means whereby mundane-experience is brought about—thus, there is no contradiction [in holding both that *bindu* and *mahāmāyā* are material causes]. Further:

(122B) When creation and maintenance have been described, destruction is [described as] the reverse process of creation.

The meaning of the verse follows: creation and maintenance are described according to their activities and according to the sequence of their genesis with respect to each *tattva*; destruction, on the other hand, is described according to how it contracts into its own causes through an inversion of the process of creation. Moreover:

(123A) Due to the beginninglessness of worldly existence, there is no permanence in the process of creation, maintenance and destruction.

The beginninglessness refers to *sāṁsārika* existence.

An objection is raised: as they provide the mean whereby mundane-experience can be brought about, creation and destruction affect souls; however, why should the Lord want to carry out destruction?

We reply: since *māyā* has the inherent power of increasing the production of the infinite mundane-experiences of the soul, the reabsorption facilitates the maturation of (souls') *karma* and also provides some rest for souls in order that they may rejuvenate their powers, just as beautiful women rejuvenate themselves in sleep. Thus, the *Mṛgendra Āgama* states: having been seized, the soul remains in order to rest. This rest is carried out for the benefit of all created beings who are the "worldlings" fatigued by the bound condition; even in this state of rest, instruction is available for those who are fit for instruction, obstruction for those who are fit for obstruction, and the maturation of karma for those who are fit for this maturation. Making the inherent powers of *māyā* fit for manifestation, the Lord watches over the whole genesis of things. (V. 4.13.-15).

Summing up that mundane-experience along with its means belongs to the soul, he is going to introduce the view that the *pāśa*, i.e., "bond", which is of the nature of *mala*, belongs solely to the soul.

> (123B-124A) The souls' "object of mundane-experience" consists of *māyā* by those means that have been produced from *māyā*. The mundane-experiencer is a defiled-soul who is conscious; the "object of mundane-experience" is not conscious.

As it has been said, the object of mundane-experience is simply a mental cognition, which is constituted by the nature of "pleasure" and so forth. This object of mundane-experience is simply an "effect" of *māyā* and is not inherent in the soul as its "quality", since the soul has consciousness intrinsic to its nature. As well, to postulate such an inherence of the mental cognition in the soul would falsely attribute mutability and so forth to the soul. In short, just the conscious soul is the mundane-experiencer of the "object of mundane-experience".

Since the soul's intrinsic consciousness and agency are obfuscated (an impure condition that will be discussed in the sequel), the soul is able to experience mundanely that which is accompanied by the *tattvas* such as *kalā* etc., which are produced from *māyā*.

But, without some cause to account for the effect, limited consciousness is not possible. How does the impurity of the soul come about? He says:

> (124B) Thus omniscience and omnipotence are obfuscated by the *mala* of the [limited] experiencer.

Although possessed by omniscience and omnipotence, like Śiva, the soul requires *kalā* etc. to limit its consciousness. Thus, not a mundane-experiencer, the released soul is said to be possessed by omniscience etc.

Therefore, given the sense of the term "mundane experiencer", the designation of [limited] "experiencer" is applied to the soul, and refers to the fact that the soul is obfuscated by *mala*. It is said that mundane-experience is a result of *mala*. Thus, the soul [with mundane-experience] is impure. The *Svāyambhuva Āgama* sates: if the soul is not impure, why does the attachment to mundane-experiences occur? (V.33.4) Thus:

> (125A) By means of the passion (*rāga*) that functions on account of *karma* in a latent condition, the soul [obfuscated by *mala*] seeks the sphere of *māyā*.

It is improper to attribute [*karmic*] development to the soul, as in the case of agricultural activities etc. Through *rāga*, which is of the nature of *karma*, the soul seeks after *māyā*, which is transformed into the means whereby mundane-experience is brought about.

During the period of the cosmic destruction at which time

the mind disappears from the *sāṁsārika* sphere due to the reabsorption of the destroyed mind into the prime matter (which is of the nature of *māyā*), mundane-experience arises due to the fructification of [the latent] *karma.*

An objection is raised:

(125B-126A) As an effect of a previous existence, *karma* provides the souls' fruits at birth etc.—why then imagine that the soul is defiled when *karma* is prevailing?

Karmic-activities [according to the opponent] cause birth, life and mundane-experience through the bondage to corporeal embodiment, which is an "effect"; this can be understood in terms of the maxim that "the seed and sprout relationship is beginningless". These *karmic*-activities develop the soul's connection to the body, which brings about the mundane-experience of the respective [*karmic*] fruits. Of what use is *mala*? After you have construed *mala* as useful [i.e., as capable of providing the souls' bondage], you go on and postulate *karma* [claiming that it is necessary], since there is nothing other to explain the variety [of the differences] of mundane-experience. Thus, you should simply designate *karma* as the cause of bondage; otherwise, your explanation is too cumbersome! The postulation of *mala* is unnecessary! Thus they say: the first account is sufficient, the second redundant! In the following verse, he refutes such an opponent:

(126B-127A) *Karma* has the power *(śakti)* to generate birth etc. But this does not take place without *mala,* as a soul that is free from impurity is nowhere to be seen.

Since it is impossible to observe either the engagement in *karmic* comportment or the actual birth of a released soul not possessed by *mala* (the actual cause of bondage) the acquisition of *karma* belongs solely to a soul possessed by *mala.* Once the accumulation of *karma* has been effected, the soul thenceforth engages in its mundane-experience.

An opponent raises a further objection: if the cause of birth etc. is *mala*, why posit *karma*?

(127B-128A) If the mundane-experiencer can be explained by one thing [i.e., *mala*] —of what use is *karma*? On account of having acquired *[mala]*, the connection to birth etc. certainly arises.

He refutes this:

(128B-129A) With respect to the released souls that have consciousness and whose existence is in no way influenced by *karma*, there is no connection to birth etc.; therefore, the cause behind mundane existence is twofold.

Since we do not see the birth etc. of the Vijñānakevalins who are free of *karma* but still impeded by *mala*, the cause of the connection to *māyā* must be twofold.

A new objection is raised: the soul cannot be obfuscated [by *mala*], since prior to the creation of the world souls possess consciousness and an intrinsic unity, like Śiva!

He disposes off this objection in the following verse:

(129B-130A) If, prior to creation, the soul is intrinsically a unified whole possessed by consciousness and agency, it cannot be subject to bondage!

If the opponent's position is accepted, the soul cannot be said to be open to a connection to *kalā*, just as Śiva is not open to a connection to *kalā*. Therefore, since there is nothing else to account for the soul's connection to *kalā*, "*mala*" ought to be postulated as belonging to the soul. Furthermore:

(130B-131A) If one postulates that consciousness and activity [inherent in the soul] have reference to all objects on account of the soul's pervasiveness, then one must also postulate that the omniscient and omnipotent soul's "state of release" is not caused by anything.

This is not the case! A cause is required, just as in the case of "limited" (i.e., "mundane") consciousness some "cause" such as *kalā* must account for this "limited" knowledge.

(131B) Just as *kalā* etc. are necessary in order to manifest the bound soul's consciousness and activity, so the released soul requires something in order to manifest its consciousness and activity.

This cannot apply to a soul that is not veiled:

(132A) The light of the sun, not being veiled, does not require a manifesting-agent.

(132b) *Mala* is a beginningless connection to [something] beginningless; it is universal and indestructible.

In this verse the "beginningless connection" refers to the "beginningless covering [by *mala*]" and "to [something] beginningless" refers to the beginninglessness of the souls; "universal" applied to all bound souls—thus one has to accept that *mala* is eternal.

The opponent raises an objection. If *mala* is eternal, there can never be a "cessation of *sāṁsārika* existence" for the soul! Or, on the other hand, if this "cessation" is accommodated, due to the supposed unity of *mala*, all souls will attain release at the time of the release of one soul. Responding to this objection, he says:

(133A) With respect to the limitations pertaining to each soul, *mala* has the power to separate the respective time [governing the respective limitations].

The innumerable powers of *mala* are restricted to individual souls. Thus, individual souls are released when their bonds qua powers [of *mala*] reach their proper maturation. In this respect, it is said that the powers are simply superimpositions *(upādhi)* over individual souls; as well, these powers reach their own end.

The opponent argues: the obfuscated condition of the soul arises as a result of the "mundane delusion" that comes about only after the creation of the world, as a result of the soul's "connection to *kalā*, etc." We reply:

(133B-134A) According to this view, the soul is considered to be unconnected to *mala* and is therefore considered to be unobfuscated, as is the case with Śiva.

However, according to the opponent's view, the soul cannot in principle abandon mundane defilement. Thus, one ought to accept the beginningless connection between the soul and the beginningless *mala*.

Furthermore:

(134B-135A) According to the wise, if the connection between *mala* and the soul has a beginning, then one must also speak about a cause [of this beginning]— and thus, an infinite regress will follow.

(135B-136A) If, on the other hand, the connection is considered to be without a cause, then even the connection to *kalā* etc. is considered to be without a cause. As a result, there will be no release for souls and there will be no lord!

If one holds that the condition fo bondage is without a cause on account of the uncaused connection to a body etc., then even the released soul will have some connection to bondage; as a result, it will be impossible for the soul to be released from the condition of bondage. Since this association to bondage would even apply to Śiva, Śiva would no longer be considered the Godhead. For these reasons, the soul's connection to *mala* ought to be accepted as beginningless and as the cause of bondage.

An opponent may claim that *mala* is manifold due to its specificity [to each soul]. According to this view, *mala* is non-eternal, due to its manifoldness and materiality, as in the case of pots etc. However, since this view postulates a type of *mala* that would have a beginning, the faults already mentioned would apply here as well, e.g., the charge of "infinite regress," "the impossibility of release", and so on. He says:

(136b-137a) If *mala* is specific [to each soul] it must be manifold, which implies that it must be unconscious. However, on account of having an origin and being subject to destruction, the earlier mentioned faults apply [to this account of *mala*].

Since *mala* is beginningless it cannot "have an end"; otherwise [if one holds that something beginningless can have an end], everything is open to destruction [i.e., all things become non-eternal].

(137B-138A) If the connection of "something beginningless to something beginningless" is established as open to destruction, then even such beginningless things as *māyā* and *Śiva* would be subject to destruction!

Having established the indestructibleness, eternality and beginninglessness of *mala,* he will now establish the fact that *mala* is possessed of endless powers:

(138B) Restricted to each soul individually, these powers of mala are the obstructors of the [soul's] qualities.

The term "qualities" in the verse refers to the soul's qualities, i.e., consciousness and activity.

Due to the failure to account, in any other manner, for the empirically observable variety of mundane-experience, this variety is therefore due to the temporal transformations of the [respective] powers of *mala.* He says:

(139A-140A) If the powers of *mala* were not temporally restrained with respect to the termination of the obstruction [of *jñāna* and *kriyā*], the simultaneous release of all those who possess consciousness would occur. Since the soul exists in a condition of beginningless obfuscation,

> *mala* is the only bond (*pāśa*) that innately coexists along with the soul.

Mala is the only bond that innately coexists along with the soul. However, the *Śvāyambhuva Āgama* and other works entertain the opponent's claim that *māyā* etc. are in fact "independent" phenomena [lacking any innate connection to the soul and *mala*]. The opponent claims that all the entities belonging to the sphere of *māyā* to which the bound soul has a connection, are solely of the nature of *māyā* itself.

In the *Mataṅga Āgama* (v. 6.103) and elsewhere this opponent is refuted on the grounds that the *mala* innately coexisting along with the soul is in fact the cause of the *mala* constitutive of delusion, passion, *rāga*, despair, etc. Thus, he says:

> (140B-141A) It is improper to hold that the five [delusions] such as madness, etc. are the [obscuring] activities of the mundane experiencer, as these five delusions never exist in souls without *kalā*.

The five delusions (which are going to be described in the sequel) are not seen when *mala* is without the connection to *kalā* etc., as in the case of the Vijñānakala and Pralayākala [souls]. The five delusions only apply to the Sakala souls. Thus, belonging to *māyā*, the five delusions do not have the function of obfuscating consciousness and activity.

The *Mataṅga Āgama* and other texts state that *mala* exists as the generating cause of the five delusions. In this case, the five delusions, which are of the nature of such mental conceptions as seeing the soul in what is not the soul, are said to have *māyā* as their material cause, because those souls that are involved in the sphere of *māyā* and that are linked to *kalā*, are not free of *mala*. Consequently, the five delusions arise on account of *mala* acting as a subsidiary cause. Only as an "associate cause" is *mala*, therefore, the cause of the five delusions. Hence, there is no contradiction in speaking of *mala* as the cause.

An objection is raised: the five delusions, whose material

cause is considered to be *mala*, are not manifested during the period of cosmic rest. They are only manifested after their connection to *kalā*.

What is wrong with this position? He says:

(141B-142B) "The five delusions are manifested on account of the connection to the means whereby mundane-experience is brought about." This is false! According to you the five delusions have the same characteristics as transformations of the *guṇas*. Thus, according to you, the five delusions are simply transformations of the *guṇas*.

He states that the manifestation of the five delusions does not arise after the connection to the means whereby mundane-experience is brought about.

An objection is raised. *Mala* is described as the cause of the five delusions. However, since *mala* is also described as eternally of the same nature, it is impossible for there to be a distinction between a manifested and an unmanifested condition of *mala*. As a result, the five delusions must be "effects" that obfuscate the soul's consciousness and activity.

No, this does not follow! Rather, the five delusions attributed to the soul are simply conditions of the internal organ and temporally arise after the soul's connection to the means whereby mundane-experience arises. Thus, the five delusions should be construed as arising from the *guṇas*, which have arisen from *māyā* together with the subsidiary cause *mala*.

He is now going to delineate the nature of the five delusions insofar as they are of the nature of the *guṇas*:

(143A-143B) Madness and delusion; attachment; despair and error—these are respectively derived from *tamas*, *sattva* and *rajas*.

An objection is raised: if the five delusions are not modifications of the *guṇas* in the condition of the internal organ, then they must be separate modifications of *mala* occurring in the soul with limited consciousness.

That this is not the case, he says:

(144A) The modifications of the cause [i.e., *mala*] are not separate from the five *guṇa*-based delusions. This is not the case!

(144B-145A) If one dismisses the powers as the obscurational factors, nothing other than mala should be acknowledged! The cause of the *"saṁskāras"* is associated with the receptacle of *karma.*

The verse points out that the ubiquitous *mala* causes the obscuration of the soul's innate consciousness and activity while the soul's connection to the *saṁskāra*-based *karmic* activity is the cause of *sāṁsārika* existence; there is no other way to explain the "effect", i.e., as the obscuration, except through positing *mala* as the cause.

Now, having delineated the innate nature of *mala*, he concludes [this verse]:

(145B) In a word, on account of its connection to mala, the soul is termed "the limited one" *(aṇu).*

In the *Raurava Āgama* and elsewhere the word "soul" *(paśu)* refers to *"mala"*. *Mala* is not a separate *tattva* from "soul" but is rather inclusive in the *"paśu-tattva"*. Without this inclusiveness of *mala* in the *"paśu-tattva"*, the bound condition *(paśutva)* of the soul cannot occur. Moreover, as a beginningless "veiling" [of the soul], the activity of *mala* is herein treated as (a) the bound soul's "mundane-experience" of "the object of mundane-experience", (b) a "diminishing" [of the soul's capacities] taking place through the *māyā*-generated forms of *kalā* etc., which act as the means whereby mundane-experience is brought about, and (c) the soul's enjoyment of mundane-experience both prior to and at the time of Śiva's creation of the world. All of the bound souls' activities arise solely on account of the obfuscation by *mala.* All obfuscational activities occur because of the existence of *mala.* Moreover, the five delusions are herein shown to be *kleśas* [sources of affliction] of the soul.

He is now going to sum up, pointing out that the differences of the activities [of these *kleśic* souls] are due to the differences in their competence. He says:

> (146A-146B) For those who are absorbed in the *tattvas,* the *kleśas* are inactive; for those who are yogins, the *kleśas* are the obstructions on the shore; for those who are addicted to worldly objects, the *kleśas* are of a manifold and developed form *(vicitra-udāra-rūpa)*

Belonging to those in the *māyā-tattva,* the *kleśas* belong to the Pralayākala souls who are limited to the *guṇa-tattva* etc. Due to their limited nature, the *kleśas* of the Pralayākala souls are "inactive", since they do not contribute towards any significant change. The *kleśas* of the yogins are manifested on account of the power of yoga; existing in the middle sphere, yogins' activities are obstructed. The ones who are attached to sense objects are the Sakala souls whose activities are diverse *(vicitra)* and developed *(udbhūta).*

If we take the reading *"vicchinna-udāra"* instead of *"vicitra-udāra"* the meaning [of the verse] becomes: for those who are addicted to worldly objects the *kleśas* are sometimes of a developed form and sometimes of an undeveloped form, because of the mutual ascendency and subjugation of the two types.

Now, having mentioned earlier that mundane-experience and release along with the means whereby they are accomplished would be treated, mundane-experience along with its means has been dealt with and the manual dealing with mundane-experience is concluded. Release along with its means will be dealt with in another manual.

In these verses the venerable guru Śrīmat Kheṭakanandana has clearly and conscisely explained mundane-experience (along with the means whereby it is brought about) according to the Śaiva Siddhānta doctrine. This unfortunately brief commentary has been written by the humble and Śiva-blessed Ācārya, Aghora Śiva.

Herein concludes the *Bhoga Kārikā*. As well, the Commentary on the Manual of Mundane Experience written by Aghora Śiva is also completed.

Endnotes

1. I have based this translation and transliteration on the edited Sanskrit text in Kṛṣṇa Śāstrī's 1923 Devakottai edition, having taken into account the suggested emendations in Vrajavallabha Dvivedī's 1988 edition of the text.
2. Sadāśiva is described as the "*bandhamokṣapranetṛ*" in RĀ, I. 1.2, p. 1.
3. Compare *Sāṁkhya Sūtra,* 3. 72: "[Bondage and Liberation belong to matter directly, because it is subject to association, like a beast] (*prakṛterañjasyātmasaṅgāt*)."
4. cf. Pandey, *Bhāskarī*, p. LXII for a discussion of the distinction between Āgamic Śaivism and Sāṁkhya.
5. A soul becomes capable of enjoying "objects of mundane-experience" when attached (*saktatva*) to mundane-experience (*bhoga*) by the *rāga-tattva,* which technically causes attachment (*anurañjaka*) to things (*viṣaya*); however, *rāga* is dependent on *mala.*

   According to Sāṁkhya, *rāga* is the cause (*hetu*) or manifester (*abhivyañjaka*) of attachment (*abhiṣanga*) which is an attribute (*dharma*) of the *buddhi.*
6. *BK* 117B-118A; the *jagadbīja* is described as the "*mahāmāyā*", which is the "*janyaśakti*" and is *acetanā.*
7. This verse is also quoted by Mādhava in the *Sarvadarśansaṁgraha* in the section dealing with *śaivadarśana;* see ed. p. 80 and trans. p. 118. The source is V. I.3.27.
8. See K. Śivaraman, *Śaivism in Philosophical Perspective,* p. 247.
9. Also quoted by Aghora Śiva in TSV on V.3.
10. A similar quotation is found in *MĀ*, p. 317: "*sthūlasūkṣmarūpatvena tānīndriyayādharāṇi sthitāni ityartham.*" The quote that follows is from V. I. 19.21.
11. Also quoted in *MĀD*, p. 317 and *MPĀ*, 19.21, p. 467; the source is *TS*, v. 4.

12. "Activities" or "modifications" are variously referred to as *vṛtti, kriyā, or vyāpāra.*
13. The subtle body (*sūkṣmadeha*) or "transference body (*ativāhika*)" is also known as the "*puryaṣṭaka*", as it consists of the five *tanmātra* and three *antaḥkaraṇa*. Elsewhere the *puryaṣṭaka* is identified with the *prāṇāṣṭaka,* i.e., that which consists of the five *prāṇa,* the *karmendriya, jñānendriya* and *antaḥkaraṇa;* cf. *Yuktidīpikā* comm. on vv. 23-24 and *Brahmasūtraśaṅkarabhāṣya* on 2.4.6. *Sāṃkhya Sūtra* 3. 7-16 claims that the subtle body (*liṅga*) is "seventeen and one"(*saptadaśaika*), which includes the three internal organs, ten organs and five subtle elements. The *Śivajñānasiddhiyār* (trans. p. 206) claims that there are actually "five" bodies, the sthūla-, sukṣma-, *guṇa-, kañcuka-* and *kāraṇa-* bodies, which the author respectively identifies with the five *kośas* of the Vedānta, i.e., the *annamaya-, prāṇamaya-, manomaya-, vijñānamaya-,* and *ānandamaya-kośa.*
14. In this context, the commentator supplies both the "gross" and "subtle" elements, whereas in the previous verse just the gross elements are discussed.
15. The commentator is attempting to explain the compound "*ativāhikadehastha*" in terms of the fact that the gross body is construed as the receptacle; therefore, the "*stha*" cannot directly be the receptacle. Moreover, the introduction of the subtle body and *karma* at this point, especially the claim in 8Ab-8B that the subtle body is only peceptible by those who have lordly powers, may be an argument against the Cārvākas who argue that the "*ceṣṭa*" is solely a product of the physical body; of the two causes the Śaivite brings forth in his explanation, i.e., *karma* and the subtle body, *karma* is *adṛṣṭa* and the subtle body is only open to the perception of those who have lordly powers.
16. *TSV,* v. 24B-25A.
17. "Spirits", i.e., "*piśācāh*"; for a description of these spirits, cf. *ŚPB,* p. 239. The Piśācas are the deities who rule over the *tattvas* from *buddhi* to earth, possess lordly powers and are of eight types.
18. A very similar description of the kramic ordering of the elements and their qualities is found in the *Mṛgendra Āgama* 12. 26-30; pp. 337-338.
19. See *MĀ,* 12. 28a; P. 338.

20. Ibid. 12. 26A, p. 337.
21. Ibid. 12. 27.
22. See *ibid.* 12. 17-19.
23. The Śaivites want to argue for a "*krama* theory" of evolutes. *Śabda* is actually a specific *guṇa* of *ākāśa* but a shared *guṇa* of the other gross elements as well; the Śaivites are arguing against the more static view of Vaiśeṣika that *śabda* is an *ekaguṇa* of *ākāśa*. Vaiśeṣika explains the presence of *śabda* elsewhere by arguing that *ākāśa* is present everywhere; see *ŚPB*, p. 283: "*svaviśeṣaguṇaḥ śabda āśrayādanyataṇ sthiteḥ heturvaiśeṣik 'yam hetvābhāso' vagamyate.*"

    Citing various Agamas, Śrīdhara argues that sound can never be a quality of any other substance, since "it is perceived elsewhere than its substratum". Sound is perceived in the ear, not in the objects which are thought to be its substratum.
24. The *hetu* is proven to be *bādhita* by some other *pramāṇa* which is stronger; it is fivefold according to the five *pramāṇas*. A typical example with respect to the *pratyakṣapramāṇa* is the statement that "fire is not hot because it is a thing".
25. According to Nyāya-Vaiśeṣika, the conception of *rūpa* is only "colour" although it signifies *form* as well, which Nyāya-Vaiśeṣika describes as *anvaya-saṁsthānviśeṣa* (a particular arrangement of parts).
26. Kṛṣṇaśāstri's Devakoṭṭai edition does not include the gross element "fire", which is corrected by Dvivedi.
27. According to the Vaiśeṣika, the five *karmendriya* fall under the category of "movement" (*karma*). According to Nyāya, the definition of the "*śarīra*" is "*ātmano bhogāyatanam*" or more specifically, *antyāvayavītve sati ceṣṭāśrayam*, a final product which possesses voluntary action.
28. Quoted in *MĀD*, p. 321; also quoted by Aghora Śiva in his commentary on v. 51 of the *Tattvaprakāśa*.
29. Cf. *TS V.* 6A: "*pratyekaṁ śabdādiṣveṣāmālocaṁ vṛttiḥ.*"
30. Cf. *TSV.* on *VV 6-7:* "*na cāyaṁ tattvāntarāṇām kāryaḥ teṣām svakāryaireva siddheḥ. kāryāntarahetutve pramāṇābhāvāt. anekatattvaparikalpanābhāvaprasaṅgācca.*"
31. *MĀV, p.* 319: "*devanāddyotanādvā devā indriyāṇi ...*"
32. A similar idea is expressed in the *MĀ*, 12.9: "when the soul, the senses, and the objects are in contact all the senses do not enter

into action. Therefore, by the same reasoning, some may infer that there is an agent which sets the senses into [their restricted] activity."

33. *MPĀ*, 18. 81-82; also quoted in *MĀD*, p. 320 (wherein "*citta*" is glossed as "*manas*" by Rāmakaṇṭha).
34. *MĀ*, p. 323.
35. Hulin translates "*abhijātamarmaraśabdavat*" as "...*craquant* agréablement (sous la dent?)"; see Hulin, *Mṛgendrāgama*, trans. p. 271.
36. The needle piercing the collection of lotus leaves is a commonly used analogy. Śrīdhara, for example, uses it to explain the quickness with which we perceive two separate objects that are perceived at the same time in different places; see *PDS*, p. 57.
37. *BK*, 117B-118A. The *jagadbīja* is "*mahāmāyā*" (which is the *janyaśakti* and *acetanatva*).
38. In the *MĀD* (p. 312), which deals with the *vāyu* "*udāna*", Aghora Śiva mentions the different kinds of *udāna* (*nāga* etc.) which are also mentioned elsewhere as "*pradhāna*", i.e., as essential forms of *vāyu*, but in fact they are, he says, secondary (*apradhāna*). He cites the *Kālottara Āgama* which lists five kinds of *udāna*, which are the same that are cited here.
39. Also quoted in *MĀV*, p. 324.
40. *Ibid.*, p. 325.
41. Quoted also in *MĀV*, p. 327.
42. Cf. Loc. cit.
43. A "Means" of apprehension may be a more appropriate term than "faculty".
44. The same quote appears in *MĀD*, p. 308 and in the *TS*, p.9, although with the more logical "*tatra yo'nadhyavasāyātmakaḥ...*"
45. *Sāṃkhya Sūtra* 3.58 and 6.40: "*prakṛti*", which is *pumārtham*, represents the sphere of the *bhogya*.
46. The whole verse appears in the *Śataratnasaṁgraha;* see p. 69 "*Bhoga* is called *vedana* and is of the nature of joy, suffering, etc.: the soul fit for this has the consciousness as due to Karma (*bhogo 'sya vedanā puṃsaḥ sukhaduḥkhādilakṣaṇaḥ tāṁ samarthitacaitanyaḥ pumanabhyeti karmataḥ*)."
47. The *MĀ* (p. 342) even attributes *cit* to the *sukṣmadeha*, thus indicating that the subtle body acts as an "intermediary" factor.

48 See *MĀ*, pp. 64-65. According to the *ŚPB* (pp. 337-339), Sāṁkhya construes *mokṣa* as "*kaivalya*", the *ātman* without adjuncts; for Nyāya it is "*uccheda*", the complete destruction of all *ātma-guṇa*; and for the Bhaṭṭas, the manifestation (*abhivyakti*) of eternal bliss (*nityasukha*).

49. *MĀ*, pp. 284-285.

50. Read this with respect to v. 55.

51. *BK*, v. 59 is quoted in *MĀD*, p. 289 as "*svacintiteṣu cāvighnorūpe...*"

52. "*Vighāta*" is not explained.

53. A similar etymology is found in the *Pauṣkara Āgama (puṃspaṭala,* v. 47; *ŚPB*, p. 232): "*ete dharmādayaśca cāṣṭau bhāvayanti*".

54. See *ŚPB*, P. 242, quoted from the *Pauṣkara* (*puṃspaṭala*, vv. 104-128): *pratyāyayanti kṣetrajñānaṁ tena te pratyayāḥ smṛtāḥ.*

55. *MĀ*, 11.12, p. 298.

56. *Yoga Sūtras*, v. 1.3.

57. *Mokṣa Kārikā*, v. 105.

58. *MĀ*, 11.12; p. 298.

59. *MĀ*, 11.6; p. 293. The *Pauṣkara Āgama* (*puṁspaṭala*, v. 120: *ŚPB*, p. 243) describes "*anaiśvarya*" as that which results from incapacity (*aśakti*), and this incapacity is of 176 kinds. Since it is often of the form of *ajñāna* and *atuṣṭi*, it is of 164 varieties; these are all incapacities of the intellect.

60. Cf. *Vedānta Sūtras*, trans. II, 272: "Nor is it true that the body is absolutely required as an auxiliary of perception – for in the state of dream the body is motionless."

61. *anyathānupapatti is arthāpatti*: presumption of some "*adṛṣṭa-artha*" to account for some "*dṛṣṭa-artha*" according to Nyāya; it is an *anumāna* which can only be proven by *vyatirekavyāpti*.

62. See *SK*, v. 20.

63. Not a quote from either the *Sāṃkhya Sūtra* or *Sāṃkya Kārikā*.

64. *Sāṁkhya Sūtra*, 6.54: "*ahaṁkāraḥ kartā na puruṣaḥ*". Aniruddha justifies this view on the basis of the position that the *puruṣa* is *apariṇamitva*: cf. also 6.55.

65. Similar quote in *MĀD*, p. 85-86.

66. *Sāṁkhya Kārikā*, p. 59.

67. Cf., for instance, Śrīdhara on *Padārthadharmasaṁgraha*; he argues that the *ātman* is neither a *bhoktṛ* nor *kartṛ* – it is wholly indifferent. Its connection to the body and the senses and the resulting

egoistic conceptions of "I" and "Mine" cause the sense of "*bhoktṛ*" and "*kartṛ*".

68. *Sāṁkhya Kārikā,* v. 37.
69. *Ibid.,* vv. 55-60.
70. *Ibid.,* v. 57.
71. *Ibid.,* v. 56.
72. *Ibid.,* v. 12.
73. *MĀ,* 10.21; p.76.
74. Quoted in *TPV* on v. 48; a similar citation is found in *MĀD* 10.11, p. 262, *TSV* on v. 4 and *MPĀ,* 11.7, p. 326.
75. See *ŚPB,* p. 201 wherein Śivāgrayogin argues that "an object of mundane-experience" is not that which causes mundane-experience; thus *karma* must be distinct.
76. Similar quote in the *MĀD,* 10.11.
77. See *ŚPB,* p. 215: the *saṁvedana* (cognition) of the *buddhi* has a distinctive *karaṇa,* since it is an act *kriyā* which thus establishes the *vidyā-tattva.*
78. *TS,* v. 14.
79. *MĀD,* p. 129 appears to be a better reading: "*apravṛttaḥ pravṛtto vā* ..."
80. See *ŚPB,* pp. 160-161 wherein limitedness implies pervasiveness: "The soul is an omniscient being veiled by something, since he is parviscient. If he were not an omniscient being vieled by something, he could not even be parviscient, like Śiva."
81. *MĀ,* 10. 7.
82. *Kalā,* not *Śivaśakti,* activities the *buddhi-tattva*; cf. Sivaraman, *Śaivism in Philosophical Perspective* (pp. 240-241): "How about *Śiva-Śakti* which is spirit itself? Can it not serve to activate the *buddhi-tattva*? The answer is that just as one's body is activated by one's own self, one's psyche too is activated by one's self alone. Because *śakti* is the cause of all effect it does not mean that it is *śakti* and not the potter that fashions the pot. It may be asked: is not *Kalā* itself *jaḍa*? Has it not to be activated by a self again? The answer to this objection is that *Kalā* and other tattvas, *jaḍa* as they are, are activated in their turn by *Śiva-tattvas* presided over by the intelligent *Śiva-Śakti.* The *Śiva-tattvas* themselves cannot take the place of *kalā-tattva* because it has been explained that the 'pure' *Śiva-tattvas* cannot function as revealers for impurity-ridden selves."

83. *RĀ*, 2.14, p. 6. In his commentary on v. 24 of the *TS*, Aghora Śiva interprets the "*ca*" in "*avyaktarāgavidyāḥ kalāsamuttāḥ kalā ca māyājā* as entailing *kāla* and *niyati*."
84. *MĀ*. 10.14.
85. *TS*, V.24-25.
86. cf. *MĀ*, 3.12.

APPENDIX

The Transliterated Text of the Bhoga Kārikā by Sadyojyoti and its Commentary by Aghora Śiva

Śrīḥ Śivābhyāṁ Namaḥ

BHOGAKĀRIKĀ

(Vṛttisahitā)

śivaṁ praṇamya sadbhogamokṣadaṁ mandacetasām
hitaya leśataḥ spaṣṭam vyākhyāsye bhogakārikām.

iha hi tatrabhavadbhiḥ sadyojyotiṣpādaiḥ prakaraṇapratipādyamānaṁ bhogamokṣātmakamarthaṁ sūcayadbhistasyaivā 'vighnaparisamāptyarthaṁprathamaṁ paramaśivanamaskāraḥ kriyate.

(1)

tribandhicitkalāyogabhogaviśleṣamokṣadam
sarvakālakramārthajñaṁ praṇamyājaṁ Śivaṁ dhruvam

trayo bandhāśca malakarmamāyālakṣaṇāste vidyante yeṣāṁ te tri-bandhinaḥ teṣāṁ tribandhinām sakalākhyānāṁ citāmātmanāṁ yo 'yaṁ kalā yogaḥ sūkṣmadehārambhakakalādipṛthivyantatattvātmakaistattadbhuvanajadeharūpaiśca māyīyairavayavaiḥ saṁbandhaḥ tena bhogaṁ tadviśleṣeṇa mokṣaṁ ca yo dadāti. tam tādṛśam.anena śivasyānādimuktatvena sarvā' nugrāhakatvam sarvakartṛtvaṁ ca sūcyate. ata eva ca sarvakālakramārthajñam sarvaṁ ca bhūtādirūpaṁ kālakramaṁ sarvāṁśca tattatkālabhāviṇaḥ padārthān jānātīti. etana ca 'sya nirmalatvāt sarvakartṛtvācca sārvakālaṁ sarvajñatā pratipādyate. kiñca, ajaṁ amalatvādeva śarīrādisambandhātmanā' pi janmanā rahitam. dhruvaṁ cāvikāriṇaṁ.na tu bindvādivat pariṇāmitvam. vikāritve jaḍatvaprasaṅgāt. śivaṁ praṇamya bhogamokṣau vacmīti vakṣyamāṇena saṁbandhaḥ.

(2)

rurusiddhāntasaṃsiddhāu bhogamokṣau sasādhanau
vacmi sādhakabodhāya leśato yuktisaṁskṛtau

sādhayanti bhogamokṣāviti sādhakā ācāryādayaḥ. teṣāṁ

dīkṣādau tatsādhanādijñānāya yuktyā anumānena saṁskṛtau pratipāditau śrīmadrauravatantropalakṣitasiddhāntaśāstre siddhau sasādhanau bhogamokṣau rauravānusāreṇaiva saṁkṣepād vadāmi. tatra tāvat satsādhanaṁ bhogaṁ. darśayituṁ bhogādhikāraḥ keṣāmityata āha.

(3)

añjanādīśanunnānāṁ jāyate bhogalolikā
karmāśayānurūpeṇa cidvatāṁ bhavamaṇḍale

malinatvādīśenādhikārāvasthena śivenānantādidvāreṇa nunnānāṁ bhogā 'bhimukhīkṛtānāmātmanāṁñjanānmalādeva hetoḥ saṁsāramaṇḍale karmasaṁskārapākānuguṇaṁ bhogalolikā bhogecchā jāyate.

nanu nirmala evā 'tmā saṁkhyairabhyupagataḥ. tadayuktam. nirmalasya bhogāsaktyasambhavāt. tatsaṁbhave vā muktasyāpi prasaṅgāt. nanu rāganibandhanā 'saktiriṣyate satyam. rago' pi malinasyaivāsaktihetuḥ. yaduktam śrīmatsvāyaṁbhuve yadyaśuddhirna puṁso' sti saktirbhogeṣu kim kṛtā iti. atha ko' sau bhogaḥ kaiḥ sādhanaiḥ sādhyate ityata āha.

(4)

īśvarecchāsamāviṣṭajagadbījaparicyutaiḥ
sādhanaiḥ sādhyate bhogo buddhivṛttyanurañjanaḥ

īśvaro 'trānanta eva tasyaiva māyākṣobhakatvāt. yaduktaṁ śrīmatkiraṇe śuddhe' dhvani śivaḥ kartā prokto 'nanto 'site prabhuḥ iti. tadicchayā kṣubdhaṁ yajjagadbījaṁ māyākhyaṁ tasmāt prasūtairasādhāraṇaḥ sūkṣmadehātmakaiḥ-sādhāraṇabhuvanādirūpaiḥ sādhāraṇā 'sādhāraṇabhuvanajadehātmabhiśca yaḥ sādhanairbhogo niṣpādyate sa ca buddhivṛttyanurañjanātmakaḥ. buddhivṛttyā sukhaduḥkhamohādhyavasāyarūpayā ātmacaitanyasya yadanurañjanaṁ sa eva bhogaḥ. anurāgaścātra sukhādhyavasāyākārabuddhivṛttiniṣṭhatayā tatsaṁvittistadanubhava eva na tu pratibimbātmatā' tmanaḥ pariṇāmitāprasaṅgāt. taduktaṁ śrīmatsvāyambhuve bhogo'sya vedanā puṁsaḥ sukhaduḥ khādilakṣaṇā iti. tatra bhūtānāṁ tāvadbhogasādhanatāṁ pratipādayati.

(5)

kṣmājalāgnimarudvyomnāṁ guṇavṛttyakṣabhūmitāḥ svamātrāpūrapuṣṭānāṁ gamayanti tadaṅgatām

atra pṛthivyādīnāṁ bhūtānāṁ ye guṇādayasta eva teṣāṁ bhogāṅgatāṁ sādhayanti. tatra guṇā gandhādayaḥ. vṛttayastu dhāraṇādayaḥ. akṣabhūmitā cendriyādhāratvam. etānyapyanantarameva darśayiṣyati. tatśca. kṣmādayo guṇairvṛttibhirakṣādhāratayā cātmanāṁ bhogasādhanatāṁ bhajantītyarthaḥ. kīdṛśāṁ kṣmādināmityata āha svamātrāpūrapuṣṭānāṁ iti. svaiḥ svaiḥ kāraṇabhūtaistan mātraiya āpūraḥ pūraṇaṁ tena pusṭānām. akṛtasya karaṇam kṛtasya parivardhanaṁ ca prakṛtikarma yataḥ. etāni ca bhūtāni svakāraṇaistanmātraiḥ saha sthūlasūkṣmatvendriyādhārāṇi sthitānītyuktaṁ śrīmanmataṅge. tanmātrāṇīha ghaṭavanmahābhūtāni lepavat iti. etatkāryam daśadhāraṇairāviśya kāryate ceṣṭām. avibhutvāt karaṇāni tu kāryamadhiṣṭhāya ceṣṭante. iti. TS, v.5 ataścaiṣāṁ sūkṣmadehasthānāṁ bhūtānāmindriyādhāratve bāhyaśarīrasthānāṁ ca diha upacaye. iti. dhātvarthagatyā dehatvena copacayadharmitve sādhāraṇe sati dhṛtyādayo 'sādhāraṇavṛttaya ityāha.

(6)

karaṇādhāradehatve dhṛtisaṅgrahapaktayaḥ vyūho 'vakāśadānaṁ ca vṛttayo vasudhādiṣu

tatra dhṛtirdhārdhāraṇam bhūmervṛttiḥ. saṅgraho' vaṣṭaṁbho' mbhasaḥ. paktiḥ pāko'gneḥ. vyūho' vayavaghaṭanaṁ vayoḥ. avakāśasyāspadasya dānamākāśasya. atha tadevaiṣāṁ sādhāraṇamindriyā- dhāratvaṁ sūkṣmadehasthatvenāha.

(7-8Aa)

ātivāhikadehasthaṁ karaṇaṁ pravijṛmbhitaiḥ yoneryonyantaraṁ cāpi yāti puṁbhogasiddhaye pumarthadādṛṣṭavaśāt

ativāhayatyātmanāṁ karma bhogena nāśayatītyātivāhikaḥ sūkṣmadehaḥ tatsthameva karaṇamindriyavargaśceṣṭate. avibhutvena nirāśraye ceṣṭānupapatteḥ. sūkṣmadehasthabhūtatanmātrādhāra evakaraṇavargaśceṣṭata ityuktam. kiñca tatsūkṣmadehasthaṁ karaṇam puruṣārthapradakarmavaśāt tasyaiva puṁso bhogasiddhye yoneryonyantaraṁ prayāti. yaduktaṁ tattvasaṃgrahe vasudhādyastattvaguṇaḥ pratipumniyataḥ kalānto'yaṃ paryaṭati karmavaśato bhuvanjadeheṣvayaṁ ca sarveṣu iti. sa ca sūkṣmadehaḥ sūkṣmatvāt piśācādivannāsmādipratyakṣaḥ. api tu yogipratyakṣagamya ityāha.

(8Ab-8B)

deho naivātivāhikaḥ
akṣādharo 'kṣagamyo 'yamanīśānāṁ piśācavat

atha bhūtānāṁ guṇānāha.

(9)

gandhaḥ kṣitau rasaḥ ṣoḍhā madhuraḥ kṣamākaban dhakah
śuklādi śuklaṁ bhāsvacca rūpaṁ kṣityādiṣu triṣu.

(10)

aśītoṣṇau mahīvayvoḥ pākajāpākajau pṛthak
jale śītaḥ śikhinyuṣṇasparśo 'yaṁ saṁvyavasthitaḥ

(11)

śabdastaddravyajanitaḥ pṛthagbhūtacatuṣṭaye
pratiśabdakasaṃghāto nabhasyevodito buddhaiḥ

tatra gandhaḥ surabhyasurabhirūpaḥ kṣitāveva. rasaḥ kṣmājalayoḥ. tatra kṣitau kaṭvamlalavaṇamadhurakaṣāyatiktarūpaḥ. jale tu madhura eva. rūpaṁ ca kṣmājalāgniṣu. tatra kṣitau śuklaraktapītakṛṣṇādyanekavidham. jale tu śuklameva. agnau bhāsvadrūpam. teṣu savāyuṣu sparśaḥ sthitaḥ. sa ca mahyāṁ vāyau ca pratyekamaśīto 'nuṣṇaḥ. kaḥ punarmahīvāyusparśayoḥ parasparaṁ bhedo 'ta āha—pākajāpākajau pṛthagiti. mahyāṁ sparśaḥ pākajaḥ. vāyau tvapākaja ityayamevānayorbhedaḥ. asya copalakṣaṇatvād rūpādayo 'pi mahīguṇāḥ pākajā eva. jale punaḥ svābhāvikaḥ sparśaḥ śīta eva. agnāvuṣṇa eva. śabdaśca bhūmyādiṣu caturṣu taistaiḥ pārthivādibhirdravyaiḥ parasparamāhatya jātaḥ. nabhasi tu pratiśrukśabdātmakaḥ.

nanu vaiśeṣikādibhirāśrayādanya-tropalabdherākāśaikaguṇaḥ śabda iṣyate. tadayuktam pratyakṣāgamabādhitatvena hetoḥ kālātyayāpadiṣṭatvāt. yataḥ śabdāśraya eva bheryādau śabdaḥ śrūyate. kiñca pṛthivyāṁ tāvat kaṭakaṭādikaḥ śabdo dṛśyate. jale chalacchalādiḥ. agnau dhamadhamādiḥ. śakaśakādirvāyau nabhasi ca pratiśabdātmaka iti.

etaccākāśaikaguṇatvam śabdasya vistareṇāsmābhirmṛgendravṛttidīpikāyāṁ pratikṣiptam. uktaṁ ca śrīmanmṛgendre iti pañcasu śabdo 'yaṁsparśo bhūtacatuṣṭaye. aśītoṣṇo mahīvāyvoḥ śītoṣṇau vāritejasoḥ.bhāsvadagnau jale śuklaṁ kṣitau śuklādyanekadhā. rūpaṁ triṣu raso' mbhassu madhuraḥ ṣaḍvidhaḥ kṣitau. gandhaḥ kṣitavasurabhiḥ surabhiśca mato budhaiḥ. iti. atha uktārthopasaṁhāraḥ.

(12A-12Ba)

ittham yathoktagandhādivrātopetā dharāvayaḥ
abhiprasiddhā lokasya

gandhādyāśrayatayā pṛthivyādayo 'rthā lokasiddhā ityarthaḥ. eṣāṁ ca bhūtānāmasmadādibāhyendriyaparicchedyaguṇatvād ghaṭādivat kāryatvasiddhestat kāraṇatayā pañca tanmātrāḥ siddhā ityāha.

(12Bb)

mātrāstairanumānataḥ

atha guṇagrahaṇādeva tadvyatirekitvād guṇino 'pi grahaṇaṁ siddhyatīti darśayituṁ proktānāṁ tāvad bhūtānāṁ guṇebhyo 'pṛthagbhāvaṁ sādhayitumāha.

(13)

citrasvabhāvakāḥ proktā guṇabhinnā dharādayaḥ
kramavaṅgyā yathā citraṁ paṭe rūpam tu veṣṭite

uktāḥ pṛthivyādayaḥ. arthād gandhādiguṇaiḥ parasparaṁ bhinnāḥ sthalopalaparvatasaritsamudrādyākārabhedena vicitrasvabhāvāśca dṛśyante. tato 'mī veṣṭitapaṭagatacitrarūpavat kramavyaṅgyā eva. nahi pṛthivyādīnāṁ paridṛśyamānāvāntarākārabhedabhinnaṁ sannikṛṣṭaṁ svarūpaṁ tadanuguṇaṁ ca viprakṛṣṭaṁ svarūpaṁ sarvaṁ.

yugapad grahītuṁ śakyam. api tvindriyairanumānena ca krameṇa vyajyate. kimataḥ ityata āha.

(14)

viśeṣaṇaviśeṣyatvavyapadeśasya dhībhidām kramavyaṅgyatvato hetorgocaratvaṁ vrajantyamī

amī dharādayo'rthāḥ kramavyaṅgyatvāddhetoḥ surabhiriyaṁ pṛthivītyādīnāṁ viśeṣaṇaviśeṣyarūpāṇāṁ dhībhidāṁ jñānabhedānāṁ tadbhāvavyapadeśasya ca viṣayatāṁ prāpnuvanti. atra ca.

(15-16A)

nāgṛhītaistu gandhādyairjātucijjāyate matiḥ dharitryāṁ hi jalādināmagrahe 'pi prajāyate. gandhādibhyastato 'nanyā jalādibhyaḥ pṛthak cabbhūḥ

hi yasmāt kāraṇāt viśeṣarūpairgandhādibhirguṇairagṛhītairviśeṣyāyāṁ dharmirūpāyāṁ dharitryām kadācidbuddhirnotpadyate. dravyāntareṣu tu jalādiṣvagṛhīteṣvapyutpadyata eva. tasmādgandhādibhyo bhūmirananyā. jalādibhyo nyaiveti. evaṁ bhūtāntareṣvapi jñeyamityāha.

(16B)

jalādiṣvevamevāyaṁ yojyo heturmanīṣibhiḥ

nanu japākusumasannidhāne raktabhāvaṁ bhajan sphaṭikamaṇiḥ śauklyaguṇagrahaṇādṛte 'pi gṛhyate. tasmādguṇigrahaṇasya guṇagrahaṇapūrvakatvamasiddhamata āha.

(17)

saṁsthānaṁ cāpi varṇaṁ ca rūpaṁ dvividhamiṣyate tasmādasiddhatā nāsti hetorupahite maṇau

iha hi dravyāṇām varṇavat saṁsthānātmakamapi rūpaṁ guṇa eveṣyate. tasmājjapākusumopahitasyāpi sphoṭikasya grahaṇam śauklyaguṇagrahaṇābhāve 'pi vṛttacaturaśrādisaṁsthānagrahaṇapurassarameva bhavatīti dravya grahaṇasya guṇagrahaṇapūrvakatvaṁ siddhameva. ato 'sya hetornāsiddhateti. ittham bhūtānāṁ bhogāṅgatvaṁ prasādhyādhunā mātrāstairanumānataḥ iti prāguktāṁ tanmātrāsiddhaṁ viśeṣayituṁ bhūtānāṁ tāvat kāryatvamanirdeśena darśayati.

(18)

guṇānāṁ kāryatāsiddhau yo heturabhidhīyate
kṣityādikakalāntānāṁ yojyaḥ kāraṇasiddhaye

guṇānāmacaitanye satyanekatvād ghaṭādivat kāranapūrvakatvam iti vakṣyati. tatastenaiva hetunā pṛthivyādīnāmapi kāryatvasiddhiḥ. tathāhi paridṛśyamānabhogavaicitryānyathānupapattyā pṛthivyādikakalāntatriṃśattattvātmakaḥ pratyātmaniyataḥ sūkṣmadeho'stītyuktam. āgameṣu ca śrūyate. tatasteṣāṁ pṛthivyādīnāṁ pratipuruṣaniyatatvenācaitanye satyanekatvāt kāraṇapūrvakatvaṁ siddhyatīti. tatra tāvad bhūtakārṇatvena tanmātrāsidsedhtattadguṇabhedādeva pṛthivyādīnāṁ kramasiddhirityāha.

(19)

śabdādyekottarādhikyā mātrāstadaviśeṣataḥ
yonayo gaganādīnāṁ kramamicchanti dharmiṇām

ayamatra tātparyārthaḥ. anabhivyaktaviśeṣaśabdamātrasvarūpaṁ śabdatanmātramākāśasyopādānam. evam tadadhovarti śabdasparśamātrasvarūpaṁ sparśatanmātraṁ vāyoḥ. śabdasparśarūpātmakaṁ rūpaṭanmātraṁ tejasah. śabdasparśarūparasātmakaṁ rasatanmātraṁ jalasya. śabdādigandhāntapañcaguṇarūpaṁ gandhatanmātraṁ bhumeriti. akṣarārthastu gaganādivacchabdādyekottaraṁ guṇādhikyaṁ yāsāṁ tāḥ śabdādyekottarādhikyāḥ. tadaviśeṣato guṇāviśeṣādanabhivyaktaviśeṣaśabdādimātrasvarūpāt teṣām gaganādīnāṁ kramād yonaya upādānabhūtāḥ śabdāditanmātrāḥ. teṣāmeva viśiṣṭaguṇayoginām dharmiṇāmākāśādīnāṁ bhūtānāṁ sṛṣṭikramamicchanti. guṇādhikhyakrameṇādho 'dhobhāvaṁ bhajantyaḥ kāryaṇāmapyadho'dhobhāvaṁ kurvantītyarthaḥ. kathaṁ punarāsāṁ bhogāṅgatvamata āha.

(20)

svakāryotpattitatpuṣṭikartṛtā sarvayoniṣu
mātrādyāsu pumarthasya sādhanatvam viniścitam

akṛtasya karaṇaṁ kṛtasya parivardhanaṁ ca yatas sarvopādānānaṁ tatastanmātrāṇāṁ māyādīnāṁ ca kāryayonīnāṁ bhogasādhanatattvotpādakatvāt tadāpūrakatayā ca bhogāṅgatvaṁ siddham. athendriyāṇāmapi bhogāṅgatvaṁ darśayituṁ prathamaṁ karmendriyasiddhamāha.

(21)

ānandagamanotsargavacanādānakarmaṇām
upasthapādapāyvasya pāṇināmāni vai pṛthak

utsargo malavirekaḥ. ānandādikriyāhetutvenopasthādīni karmendriyāṇi siddhānītyarthaḥ. kimetānyupasthādīni sthānānyevendriyāṇi netyāha.

(22)

bhāvābhāvau tu yattantrau pratyekaṁ karmaṇām smṛtau
sthāneṣu satsu tānīha pañca karmendriyāṇi tu

iha hi keṣāñcit pādādisthānayogināmapi tattadindriyaśaktihīnānāṁ gamanādikriyā na dṛśyate. tasmātteṣu sthāneṣu satsvapi tāsāṁ kriyānāṁ yadadhīnau bhāvābhavau tāstatrasthāḥ śaktaya eva pṛthak pañcendriyāṇi jñeyāni. ata eva karmendriyāṇi yenecchanti naiyāyikādayaste pratikṣiptāḥ. nanvevaṁ ced bhṛūlatotkṣepādīnāmapi kriyātvādanantatā karmendriyāṇāṁ prasajyate. ata āha.

(23)

ānandādibhiretaistu karmabhiḥ paribhāṣitaiḥ
karmendriyāṇyato naiṣāṁānantyaṁ karmaṇām vaśāt

bhavedayaṁ doṣo yadyasmābhiḥ śarīraikadeśavṛttīni tānīṣyante. tvagindriyavat teṣāṁ sarvaśarīravyāpakatvene -ṣṭatvāddhastasyaivāyaṁ bhrūkṣepaṇādivyāpāraḥ. pāyvāderiva jīrṇavirecanādyātmaka iti bhrūkṣepādīnāmapyānandādiṣvevāntarbhāvānna tadbhedādatrendriyānantyasiddhiḥ. kiñcaitaireva ānandādibhiḥ prāguktaiḥ pradhānabhūtaiḥ karmabhiḥ pañcaiva karmendriyāṇi sidhyantīti nānantatā karmendriyāṇāṁ tattatsaṁjñāstu teṣām tatra tatra viśeṣādhiṣṭhānādityavirodhaḥ. idānīṁ buddhīndriyasiddhamāha.

(24)

śabdādigrahaṇe puṁsaḥ karturnākaraṇā kṛtiḥ
na caikarkaraṇā yasmādapekṣā na nivartate

śabdādigrahaṇasyāpi kriyātvācchidikriyāyavat karaṇaṁ vinā notpattiṛyuktā. na ca tāḥ pañcāpi kriyāḥ śtrotrāderekasmādeva karaṇādutpadyante. yasmāt karaṇāntarāpekṣā na nivartate śabdagrahaṇakaraṇabhūte śrotre satyapi sparśādigrahaṇe tvagādikaraṇāntarāpekṣitā dṛśyata iti bhāvaḥ.. kāni tāni karaṇānītyata āha.

(25A)

karaṇāni śtrutistvak ca cakṣurjihvā ca nāsikā

tataśca śabdādigrahaṇānyathānupapattyā tānyanumīyante ityabhiprāyenāha.

(25B)

śabdādyālocanaṁ teṣām vṛttiḥ śabdādisannidhau

sannibheti pāṭhe śabdādibāhyākārasadṛśamāntaramākāramadhyavasāyinyā buddhyā saha mano 'dhiṣṭhitānīndriyāṇi vidyāyā viṣayatvenopasthāpayantītyarthaḥ. taṁ cendriyopasthāpitaṁ buddhyādhyavasitamākāramantaraṅgeṇa vidyākhyena karaṇena purṣo gṛhṇatīti vakṣyāmaḥ. uktaṁ cānyatra. buddhyādhyavasitamarthaṁ puruṣaścetayate iti. na caitāni karṇaśaṣkulyādisthānānyevendriyāṇi. api tu tatsthāḥ śaktaya eva yataḥ sthānavatāmapi karmavaśāt tacchaktivaikalyānna śabdādijñānamutpadyata ityāha.

(26)

etāni sthānamātrāṇi bhuddhyakṣānīti mā kṛthāḥ
sthāneṣu satsu vaikalyānna saṁvijñāyate yataḥ

athāntaḥkaraṇasiddhirucyate.

(27)

icchāsaṃrambhabodhākhyā noktaiḥ siddhyanti sādhanaiḥ.
tatsiddhau karaṇānyantarmano 'haṅkārabuddhayaḥ

iha hi pṛthivyādīnāṁ tattvānāṁ svakāryaireva siddheḥ kāryāntarahetutve pramāṇābhāvād anekatattvaparikalpanābhāvaprasaṅgācca yānīcchādisiddhau sādhanāni tāni manohaṅkārabuddhyākhyānyāntarāṇi karaṇānītyantaḥkaraṇasiddhiḥ.tatrecchāśabdenaikāgratāparaparyāyo' vadhānātmakaḥ saṅkalpo vivakṣitaḥ. sa manaso vṛttiḥ. saṁrambhaśca prayatnohaṅkārasya. bodhaścādhyavasāyo buddheriti. etacca prapañcayiṣyate. eṣām cāntaḥkaraṇabahiṣkaraṇānāṁ parasparopakāreṇa puruṣārthasādhanatvamāha.

(28)

antarmukhāni bāhyāni saṁbhūyecchādisādhanam
śibikodvāhinaravadekāpāyena tāstataḥ

(29)

antarmukhāgatānāṁ ca citerarthaṁ prakurvatām
bāhyārthaṁ buddhibhiḥ sārdhaṁ na syuricchādikāḥ kriyāḥ

yato'ntarmukhāni bāhyāni ca karaṇāni śibikodvāhinaravat saṁbhūyecchādīnāṁ kriyāṇām sādhanaṁ bhavanti. bāhyārthālocanapūrvāṇāmeva'dhyavasāyādīnāṁ darśanāt avadhānādinā vinā bāhyārthagrahaṇāsaṁbhavācca. tataściterātmano'rthaṁ bhogākhyaṁ prayojanaṁ sādhayatāmantaramukhāgatānāmantaḥkaraṇānāṁ caśabdād bahiṣkaraṇānāṁ vā 'nyatarasyāpi vargasyāpāyena tiṣṭhatāṁ satāṁ tā icchādikāḥ kriyāḥ śabdādibāhyārthabuddhayo vā puruṣārthasādhanatayā notpadyante. yathā śibikodvāhinormadhyādekasyāpāye tadudvahanakriyā na dṛśyate. atra parābhiprāyamāha.

(30A)

anyentaḥkaraṇaṁ prāṇamicchanti vyaktacetanam

anye lokāyataikadeśāḥ praṇayanādivṛttibhirjīvanādih etubhūtaṁ bhūtapariṇāmaviśeṣādabhivyaktacetanaṁ prāṇākhyamāntaraṁ vāyumevāntaḥkaraṇamāhuh. asya dūṣaṇamāha.

(30B)

prayatnairna vinā so 'sti tatsiddhau karaṇaṁ tu kim

prāṇātmanastāvad vāyoḥ kādācitkatvena prayatnapūrvikā

pravṛttirdṛśyate. yadāhuh preraṇākarṣena vāyoḥ prayatnena vinā kutaḥ iti. tataḥ saṃrambhātmakaprayatnasiddhau kenāpi karaṇena bhāvyamityantaḥkaraṇasiddhiḥ. vakṣyati ca saṁrambho 'haṁkṛtervṛttiḥ iti. kiñca caitanyotpattirapyasya vāyorbhavatā bhyupagateti tasyāḥ karaṇāntaraṁ vācyamityāha.

(31)

caitanyodgārabhāro 'yamasyāntaḥkaraṇaṁ vada
vyaktaṁ na cāsya caitanyaṁ vāyutvād bāhyavāyuvat

na jaḍasya caitanyābhivyaktiryuktā sarvasya caitanyābhivyaktiprasaṅgādityasya na caitanyaṁ vāyutvād bāhyavāyuvaditi. itthaṁ prānāntaḥkaraṇapakṣaṁ nirasya prāguktādantaḥkaraṇatrayānmanaḥ sādhanāyāha.

(32)

icchāhetvāśu sañcārī bāhirdevapravartakam
mano yasyāśubhāvācca karturna yugapanmatiḥ

devanād dyotanād devaśabdenendriyāṇyucyante. matiśabdena ca tattadarthaviṣyaṁ jñānam. tataścāyamarthaḥ. iha hyātmano indriyārthasannikarṣe satyapi sarvāṇīndriyāṇi yugapanna pravartante. kiñcideva na ca tatsarvadā pravartate. tatastatpravṛttau yatkaraṇam tadicchāyāḥ saṅkalpātmano' vadhānasya hetubhūtaṁ bāhyendriyapravartakaṁ ca mano boddhavyam. ata eva ca tadāntareṇa antaḥkaraṇādhiṣṭhānena sukhādisaṅkalpena ca bāhyendriyādhiṣṭhānena ca dvidhā' dhikārītyuktam. śrī manmataṅgedvidhā 'dhikāri taccittaṁ bhokturbhogopapādakam. bahiṣkaraṇabhāvena svocitena yataḥ sadā. indriyāṇāṁ tu sāmarthyaṁ saṅkalpenātmavartinā. karotyantaḥsthitaṁ bhūyastato'ntaḥkaraṇaṁ manaḥ. iti. śrīmanmṛgendre 'pi. devapravartakam śīghnacāri saṅkalpadharmi ca manaḥ. iti. nanu svāduśurabhyabhijātamarmaraśabdavadabhirūpadīrghataraśaṣkulyāsvādane yugapat pañcajñānotpattirdṛśyate. tanna. yatastatrāpyutpalapatraśatavyaktibhedavadlakṣyasūkṣma kramāṇyeva pañcajñānānyutpadyante. ata eva etadāśu saṃcārītyuktam. evamahaṅkāramapi sādhayati.

(33A-33Bb)

pañcakarmakṛto vāyorjīvanāya pravartakaḥ saṃrambho'haṅkṛtervṛttiḥ

jīvanāya śarīradhāraṇārthaṁ praṇayanāpanayanādipañcakarmakṛtastattadvṛttibhedena prāṇāpānādisaṃjñābhājo vāyoḥ pravartakaḥ saṁrambhātmako yaḥ prayatnaḥ so' haṅkāravṛttirityahaṅkārasiddhiḥ. yaduktaṁ śrīmanmṛgendre-atha vyaktāntarād buddhergarvo'bhūt karaṇam citah. saṁrambhād yasya ceṣṭante śārīraḥ pañca vāyavaḥ. iti. tatra praṇayanaṁ sūkṣmadehasyordhvādhonayanaṁ prāṇasya vyāpāraḥ. apanayanamadhaḥprāpaṇaṁ malāderapānasya. annādeh rasarūpasya sarvagātreṣu sāmyena nayanaṁ samānasya. vinamanamaṅgānāṁ vyānasya. unnayanamāntarasya dhvanervarṇatāprāpaṇamūdānasya pañcakarmakṛta iti ca prādhānyāduktam. udgārādikartṛtvena cāsya vāyoḥ śravaṇāt. yaduktaṁ śrīmatkālottare-udgāre nāga ityuktaḥ kūrma unmīlane sthitaḥ. kṛkarastu kṣute caiva devadatto vijṛmbhaṇe. dhanañjayaḥ sthito poṣe mṛtasyāpi na muñcati. kiñca buddhikāryādayam ghaṭa ityādigrāhyādhyavasāyarūpāt pratyarthaṁ bhinnarūpāt pratyayādatyantabhedena bhāsamānaḥ sarvārthagrahaṇe'pyekarūpo'hamiti grāhakādhyavasāyarūpaḥ pratyayo 'haṅkārasyaiva vṛttirityāha.

(33Bb)

anyo 'rthapratyayo paraḥ

ahaṅkāravṛttyātmakapratyayo'rthapratyayādanya ityarthaḥ. nanu śabdagrahaṇādayaḥ śrotrādināma-sādhāraṇavṛttayaḥ saṁrambhastu teṣāmevendriyāṇāṁ sādhāraṇavṛttiriti kimanyenāhaṅkāreṇa kalpitena. ata āha.

(34)

na devagrāmasāmānyavṛttiḥ saṁrambha iṣyate yato 'nyatamavaikalye jāyate satyahaṅkṛtiḥ

sādhāraṇakāryakartṛnāmekāpāye tatkriyānutpatteruktatvāt tadvaikalye 'pi jāyamāno 'yam saṁrambho 'haṃpratyayo vāhaṅkārasyaiva kārya ityarthaḥ. atraiva prasaṅgād buddhīndriyakarmendriyatanmātravargānāṁ manaḥsahitā-nāmahaṅkārādevotpattiriti darśayitumāha.

(35)

anye cāhaṅkṛtiskandhāstrivargajanakāstrayaḥ
taijasādikanāmānaḥ kramaśaḥ sāttvikādayaḥ

sattvarajastamobahulāḥ sāttvikarājasatāmasāstrayo' haṅkāraskandhāḥ kramāt taijasavaikārikabhūtādikasaṃ-jñābhājo bhavanti. sāttvikāditvaṁ caiṣām sattvādiguṇabāhulyāṭ nāmiśraṁ pariṇamata iti nyāyena guṇāntarasaṃsargo 'pyeṣāṁ vidyate yataḥ. tatra kutaḥ keṣāmutpattirityata āha.

(36)

samano buddhidevānāṁ guṇo yasmāt prakāśakaḥ
tasmāt sa sāttvikājjātaḥ svānurūpādahaṅkṛtaḥ

atra naiyāyikamatamanūdya dūṣayati.

(37)

anye tu buddhidevānāṁ bhautikatvaṁ prapedire
viṣayānāṁ tu niyamādasiddhādeva hetutaḥ

evaṁ hi te manyante. śabdaikagrāhakaṁ śtrotam sparśaikagrāhika tvagityādiniyataviṣayatvādindriyāṇāṁ tāni śabdādyādhārākāśādibhūtajanyāni. āhaṅkārikatve tu teṣāmekakāraṇatvādekarūpatā syānna tu pratyekaṁ viṣayaniyamasiddhiriti. tadidam tairasiddhādeva hetoḥ kalpyate. teṣām viṣayaniyamasya prakṛtiniyamasādhakasyā' siddheḥ. niyataviṣayatve hīndriyāṇāṁ tāni svasvakāraṇānyeva bhūtāni guṇasahitāni gṛhṇīran. yāvatā dravyāntarāṇi tu tadguṇāśca cakṣurādinā gṛhyate. tathāhi.

(38)

caturdravyagatān sparśāṁṣcaturo mārutā tvacā
dravyāṇyaniyataṁ caiva gṛhṇāti marutā samam

tvagindriyaṁ tāvad vāyavyatvenā 'bhyupagataṁ vāyusahitāni pṛthivyaptejāṁsi tadgatāṃsca sparśān gṛhnāti. kim ca.

(39)

trīṇi dravyāṇi cakṣuśca teṣu rūpāṇi caiva hi
ato na niyamo 'kṣāṇāṁ viṣayāṇāṁ ca kalpyate

dūṣaṇāntaramāha.

(40)

bhautikatvācca niyame karmasāmānyayoḥ sphuṭam
devebhyo buddhayo na syuḥ samavāye ca dehinām

bhautikatvasādhanāyā 'kṣāṇāṁ viṣayaniyame 'bhyupagamyamāne bhūtebhyo guṇebhyaśca vyatirekeṇa bhavadbhirabhyupagatānāṁ karmasāmānyasamavāyānāṁ padārthānāṁ buddhayastebhyo jāyamāna na bhaveyuḥ. yadapyuktamāhaṅkāritve tulye kathamakṣāṇāṁ kāryabheda iti tadapyutpattibhedādikṣuvikārāṇāṁ guḍakhaṇḍaśarkarādīnāmivabhaviṣyatīti matvā śrotrādīnām śabdādigrahaṇaniyāmakāpekṣāyāmapyasmābhiḥ puruṣārthadāyakaṁ karmaiva niyāmakamiṣyata ityāha.

(41)

na cāpyahaṅkṛto janma niyame kāraṇaṁ mama
pumarthadātṛ yatkarma kāraṇaṁ tat bhaveritam

nāsmābhirahaṅkārajatvameva viṣayaniyame kāraṇamiṣyate. kintu śivādhiṣṭhitaṁ karma cetyarthaḥ. kāyarandhraviśiṣṭe nabhobhāge śabdāvadyotake 'bhyupagamyamāne nāsārandhrādīnāmpi śravaṇendriyatvaprasaṅgatayā śravaṇākāśasyaiva śabdagrāhakatvaniyame karmaivā' dṛṣṭākhyaṁ niyāmakaṁ bhautikendriyavādinā' pi iṣyata ityāha.

(42)

nānāśrutibhayāt klṛpte sve pareṇāpi kāraṇam
śabdabhogasya niyame tatpradaṁ karma bhāṣitam

sve kāyākāśe śabdagrāhake kalpyamāne nānāśrutitvaprasaṅgabhayācchravanākāśasyaiva śabdagrahaṇaṇiyame puruṣārthapradaṁ karmaiva kāraṇaṁ bhavatā 'pīṣyata ityanvayaḥ. ittham karmendriyāṇāmāhaṅkārikatvamāha.

(43)

rājasād vaikṛtād vargaḥ karmākṣāṇāṁ tu karmakṛt
jātaḥ kāryasya yeneha kāraṇānuvidhāyitā

rajasaḥ pravṛttihetutvād rājasād vaikārikākhyādahaṅkāraskandhāt kriyāhetuḥ karmendriyavargo jātaḥ yasmāt kāraṇānuvidhāyitvaṁ kārye dṛśyate. ata eva sattvasya prakāśatvāt prakāśasya buddhīndriyavargasya sāttvikādutpattiruktā. anyathā bhinnasvabhāvaoranayorvargayorekasmādevotpattyabhyupagame kāraṇāniyamalakṣaṇo 'navasthādoṣaḥ prasajyate ityāha.

(44)

vinivārayituṁ śakyā nāvyavasthā vikārajā
sāttvikāt saṃbhave klṛpte sāttvarājasavargayoḥ

ata eva

(45)

mātrāsaṅgho 'pyahaṅkārādvargadvayavilakṣanaḥ
prakāśyastāmasastasmājjāto 'bhūtādisaṃjñakāt

idānīm buddheradhyavasāyādihetutvamāha.

(46)

prakāśo viṣayākāro devadvāro na vā kvacit
puṃbodhavyaktibhūmitvād bodho vṛttirmatermatā

indriyadvāro 'yaṁ ghaṭa ityādibāhyaviṣayādhyavasāyarūpaprakāśastadanapekṣaścāntarasmṛtipratibhādiprakāśo vāśabdād vakṣyamāṇo bhāvapratyayalakṣaṇaśca prakāśaḥ puruṣabodhasya vyaktisthānatvād bodhākhyo materbuddhervṛttirjñeyā. tato 'dhyavasāyasmṛtyādiliṅgā buddhiḥ siddhyatīti. taduktam śrīmanmṛgendre iti buddhiprakāśo 'yam bhāvapratyayalakṣaṇaḥ. bodha ityucyate bodhavyaktibhūmitayā paśoḥ. iti. eva cabuddhibodhastrividha ityāha.

(47Aa)

klṛptirmatiḥ smṛtiśceti

tatra klṛptiḥ kalpanaṁ pratibhetyarthaḥ. matiśca mananaṁ

jñānamadhyavasāya iti yāvat. itthamicchādikāryabhedādantaḥkaraṇabhedaḥ siddha ityupasaṃharati.

(47Ab-47B)

jātā bhinnārthavācakāḥ
icchāsaṃrambhabodhakhyāstenāntaḥkaraṇaṁ tridhā

smṛtyādīnāmavāntarabhede 'pi bodhakatvenaikārthatvāt buddhivṛttitvam icchādayastu vṛttayo bhinnārthatvād bhinnakāraṇā iti bhāvaḥ. nanu pṛthivyādīnāṁ viṣayatvena bhogyatvādindriyāṇām ca tadgrahaṇahetutvādastu bhogasādhanatā. buddhestu indriyārthasannikarṣādātmanyutpadyāmanāyāḥ saṃvedanarūpatvānna bhogasādhanatā. api tvātmaguṇataiveti naiyāyikādayaḥ. ata āha.

(48)

tulye guṇānvitatve tu saṁvedyaṁ kiñcidiṣyate
buddhiścāpi hyasaṃvedyā dhanyā tārkikatā tava

ayamabhiprāyaḥ dvividho 'tra bodho 'dhyavasāyātmako' nadhyavasāyātmakaśca.tatra yo 'dhyavasāyātmakaḥ sa sarvadā grāhakarūpeṇaiva bhāsamānatvādātmanaḥ svabhāva eva. yastvanadhyavasāyarūpaḥ sa utpattyapavargayogitvena bhāsamānatvānna puṁsaḥ svabhāvaḥ. nityasyānityasvabhāvatvāyogāt. tatsvabhāvatve cānityatvaprasaṅgāt. na ca nityo 'nubhūyate. tato na puṁsaḥ svabhāva iti. yasya saḥ svabhāvaḥ sā buddhirbhābhvānāmadhyavaseyatotpādikā dharmajñānādyaṣṭaguṇā buddhiriti. tataśca viṣayādhyavasāyarūpatvād bhāvapratyayātmanā sattvādiguṇatrayānvitena svarūpena bhogyatvācca buddherapi saṃvedyataiva. na tvātmaguṇatvam. taduktaṁ tattvasaṁgrahe buddhirviṣayākāra sukhādirūpā samāsato bhogyam iti. prayogaścātra bhavati buddhirapi saṁvedyaiva sattvādiguṇānvayāt pṛthivyādivaditi. karaṇatvaṁ cendriyavadasyā viṣayādhyavasāyahetutvāt siddhamityuktam. nanu dharmādīnāṁ bhāvānāmapyasmābhirātmaguṇatvamiṣyate. tadayuktam. teṣāmātmasaṁskārakatvāyogāt. tathāhi. jyotiṣṭomādikarmasaṃskārastāvannātmani saṁbhavati, avikāritvāt karmaṇāṁ ca kṛṣyādināmātmasaṁskāratvādṛṣṭeḥ, api tu jaḍa eva. yatra tāni saṁskāraṁ kurvanti sā buddhiḥ.

evaṁ jñānādisaṁskāre 'pi vācyam. tadbalādeva svapnasmṛtipratibhādāvasatyapyarthe ullekho dṛśyate. yataḥ ataśca.

(49)

antarbahiśca karaṇaṁ sākṣād bhogasya sādhanam
bhogyaṁ vinā na bhogo 'stī tyato bhogasya sādhanam

āntaro bāhyaśca karaṇagrāmo bhogasya sukhaduḥkhādisaṁvedanātmaṇaḥ sākṣāt karaṇaṁ. yaduktaṁ śrīmatsvāyambhuve bhogo 'sya vedanā puṁsaḥ sukhaduḥkhādilakṣaṇā iti. sa ca bhogaḥ srakcandanādibhogyaṁ vinā na syāditi tadgrahaṇapūrvakasya sukhādyadhyavasāyasyāpi sādhanamiṣyate. etadeva dṛṣṭāntena prakaṭayati.

(50)

sainikān vijayāyeha prayuṅkte nṛpatiryathā
prayuṅkte mahadādīni bodhādyarthamaṇustathā

(51)

sainikasthe jaye rājñaḥ kartṛtvam tu yathā tathā
buddhyādisaṃsthe bodhadau puṃsaḥ kartṛtvamiṣyate

(52)

svātmārthaṁ sainikānāṁ tu vijayo neti te yathā
sādhanaṁ vijayasyeṣṭāstathaiva mahadādayaḥ

(53A)

teṣāmapi hi bodhādyaṁ svārthaṁ neti viniścitam

karaṇānāmacetanatvāt tadvṛttīnāṁ na svārtham. api tu cetanapuruṣārthataiveti bhāvaḥ.

(53B)

tato bodhādivṛttīnāṁ sādhanaṁ mahadādayaḥ

adhunā bhogyaṁ vibhajati.

(54)

mohaduḥkhasukhākāro rūpākhyastadbhavo dvidhā
baudho bodhaḥ paraṁ bhogyaṁ māyādi ca tadarthataḥ

udbhūtaguṇatvena mohādihetutvānmohādyākāro rūpasaṃjño dharmādibhāvavargaḥ tadupādānaḥ siddhyādipratyayavargaśca dvidvidho 'yaṁ bauddho bodhaḥ puṁsaḥ paramavyavahitaṁ bhogyaṁ māyādikaṁ bhuvanādivastu tadanvayatastadarthatvādbhogādhikaraṇatvāt paraṁparayā bhogyamiti. ko 'sau rūpākhya ityata āha.

(55)

adharmāditrayaṁ rāgo dharmādi ca catuṣṭayam
tamorajaḥ sattvamayaṁ rūpaṁ tatkarmajaṁ matau

adharmājñānānaiśvaryākyaṁ rūpaṁ tāmasaṁ rāgastvavairāgyākhyaṁ rājasaṁ dharmajñānavairāgyaiśv-aryākhyaṁ sāttvikamityevamaṣṭavidhaṁ rūpaṁ buddhau guṇatvena sthitaṁ karmataścopādānājjātam. tattvabhu-vanaśarīrādi tu karmaṇaiva sahakāriṇa māyākhyādupādānāt sākṣāt paraṁparayā cotpannamityuktaṁ śrīmatsvāyambhu-vādau. ete ca.

(56)

atyantocchedato muktāvabhivyakteśca sarvataḥ
paṭādibodhāvaitatyādātmano na guṇā guṇāḥ

yato dharmādīnāṁ mokṣe 'tyantocchedaḥ parairapīṣyate yataścātmasvabhāvasya jñānakriyātmano nityasya vyākpakasya muktau sarvato vyāpakatvenābhivyaktiḥ śrūyate yasmācca paṭadijñānāmadhyavasāyarūpaṇāmavaitatyamavyāpakatvaṁ dṛśyate. tasmādanityā avyāpakāścādharmādayo nityasya vyāpakasyātmano guṇā bhavituṁ nārhanti. tatsamavāye tasya pariṇāmitvādidoṣaprasaṅgāt. ete cādharmādayaḥ sāṃsiddhikavainayikaprākṛtabhedāt trivdhā ātmana utpadyante. yaduktaṁ śrīmanmṛgendre sāṃsiddhikā vainayikā prakṛtāśca bhavantyaṇoḥ. viśiṣṭadharmasaṃskārasamuddīpitacetasāṁ. gunaḥ sāṃsiddhiko bhāti dehāpāye 'pi pūrvavat. lokadhīguruśāstrebhyo bhāti vainayiko guṇaḥ. samārjito vainayiko manovāktanuceṣṭayā. prākṛto dehasaṃyoge vyaktaḥ svapnādibodhavat. iti. ataścaivaṁ trividhebhyo dharmādibhyaḥ phalabhedānāha.

(57)

eṣāmadhogatirbandho vighātaḥ saṁsṛtiḥ kramāt
svargo muktiḥ prakṛtibhāvo vighātaśca phalāni ca

(58)

bhavaḥ sthānāparādho 'tha vighno bhogānatikramaḥ

vaśyordhvasthitiḥ saddṛṣṭibhṛtvaṁ bhogāspṛhā phalam
(59)
svacintiteṣu vā vighno rūpe sāṃsiddhike phalam
vinayaprakṛte rūpe pūrvoktaphalasaṁgrahaḥ

vainayikebhayaḥ prākṛtebhyaścādharmādibhyaḥ kramādadhogatyādīni phalāni bhavanti. sāṃsiddhikebhyastu bhavādīni. tatrā 'dhogatirnarakaprāptiḥ. bandho 'nātmanyātmābhimānitādiḥ. saṃsṛtistiryagādiyoniprāptiḥ. muktiśca darśanāntarmokṣaḥ. paramukterdīkṣāphalatvena mokṣakārikāsu vakṣyamāṇatvāt. prakṛtibhāvaḥ prakṛtilayaḥ. bhavaḥ saṁsāraḥ. sthānāparādhaḥ svasthānānnyakkāraḥ. bhogānatikramo bhogecchā. vaśyordhvasthitiḥ vaśyānāṁ svapadādhaḥsthānināmadhiṣṭhānām. saddṛṣṭibhṛtvaṁ tattadviṣayasamyagjñānayogaḥ. śeṣam sugamam. ittham bhāvān vicārya pratyayān vyāceṣṭe.

(60)
vyaktāvyaktajñasaṁbuddhiḥ siddhiḥ saṁprati siddhyati
rāgamātrānuliptāṅgād dharmādisamudāyataḥ

iha hi buddhau vāsanātvena sthitā dharmādayo 'ṣṭau bhāvā ucyante. yadāhuḥ bhāvayanti yato liṅgaṁ tena bhāvāḥ prakīrtitāḥ iti. ta eva prakarṣāvasthāṁ prāptāḥ sthūlena rūpeṇa bhogyadaśāmāpannāḥ saṁsāriṇāṁ pratyāyanāt pratyayāḥ kathyante. taduktam pratyāyayanti kṣetrajñaṁ pratyayāstena kīrtitāḥ. iti. ataśca vairāgyena rājaseneṣadyuktāt sāttvikād dharmādibhāvacatuṣṭayāt siddhirutpadyate. sā ca vyaktasya guṇāderavyaktasya ca pradhānasya jñasya ca puruṣasya saṁbuddhistadviṣayṁ jñānameva prakarṣāvasthāṁ prāptā siddhirucyate. uktaṁ ca puṁprakṛtyādiviṣayā buddhiryā siddhiratra sā. iti. tatra vyaktāvyaktaviṣaye buddhibodhe tatprakāśakatvenātyantaṁ viviktaḥ puruṣaḥ svayamevāvabhāsate. yadāhuḥ tadā draṣṭuḥ svarūpe 'vasthānaṁ iti. na tu buddhiprakāśyatayā yogyatvādidoṣaprasaṅgāt. bhogyatvādidoṣaprasaṅgāḍ. yadvakṣyati mokṣakārikāsu pariṇāmī pumān bhogyaḥ prāptastadgocaro yadi. iti.

(61)

dharmādirūpasaṃpṛktā pāpāditrityodbhavā
tuṣṭiḥ kṛtārthavijñānamanayā 'tmagrahe sati

sāttvikairdharmādibhirīṣatsaṃpṛktādadharmāditrayāt tāmasāt tuṣṭirutpadyate. sā ca tuṣṭiḥ prāguktayā bhūtatanmātrādijñānarūpayā siddhyā tattaddarśnoktena svarūpeṇātmano grahaṇe sati. adhastanaviṣayād vairāgyādakṛtārthasyāpi kṛtārtho 'smītyutpadyamānā buddhistuṣṭirucyate. yacchrūyate tuṣṭirnurakṛtārthasya kṛtārtho 'smīti yā matiḥ. iti.

(62)

adharmāditrayājjātā rāgaleśānurañjitāt
aśaktirdevavaikalyādasāmarthyaṁ śubhādiṣu

śubhaśabdenātropasthendriyavyāpara āhlāda ucyate. tadādiṣu indriyavaikalyāt tadupalakṣitaśarīravaikalyādvā klaibyabādhiryadirūpaṁ yadasāmarthyaṁ seymaśaktistāmasād vargād rājaseneṣatsaṁpṛktād bhavati. uktaṁ ca aśaktirapravṛttatvāt tāmasī duḥkhabhāvataḥ. rājasyāpi guṇo dṛṣṭaḥ kārye kāraṇasaṃśrayaḥ. iti.

(63)

tasmādevāyathāvastu vijñānaṁ vītarāgataḥ
īṣad dharmādisaṁpṛktādabhivyakto viparyayaḥ

tasmāt tāmasavargād rājasahīnāt sāttvakateṣadyuktādayathārthagrahaṇarūpo viparyayastamo mohamahāmohatāmisrāndhatāmisralakṣaṇo jāyate. yacchrūyate kiñcitsāmānyato 'nyatra matiranyā viparyayaḥ. iti. itthamatisaṃkṣepeṇoktaṁ bhāvapratyayātmakaṁ buddhibodhamupasaṁharati.

(64Aa)

leśokto buddhidharmo 'yaṁ

eṣām ca bhāvapratyayānāṁ prapañcaḥ śrīmanmataṇgādau vistareṇa darśitaḥ. prakāśitaścāsmābhirmṛgendravṛttidīpikāyāmiti tata evāvadhāryaḥ. gandhavistarabhayāttu nātra likhyate. ayaṁ ca.

(64Ab)
cetanenopabhujyate

bhogyatvāditi śeṣaḥ. bhogyatvameva sādhayati.

(64B-65A)
bhogyatvaṁ cāsya saṃsiddhaṁ yenotpanno' nubhūyate
sa cāpyanubhavo bhogo bhoktāraṁ gamayatyalam

asya bauddhasya jñānasyotpattyapavargayogitvena bhogyatvameva na tu bhoktṛtvaṁ tasya sarvadā grāhakarūpeṇa sthirasyaiva svasaṁvedanasiddhatvādatyuktam. ataśca.

(65B)
sādhayitrā vinā yasmāt siddhirneha samīhitā

iha hi buddhicaitanyavādibhirbaudhairbhoktṛtvenābhyupagatasyāsya bauddhasya jñānasyāsthiratvena ghaṭādivadacetanatvāt kālāntarabhāvikarmaphalabhoktṛtvāsaṁbhavāduktavadbhogyatvācca sa tattadviṣayasukhādyanubhavarūpo bhoga eva bhoktāraṁ sādhayati. yato bhogakriyāsiddhirbhoktāraṁ ceṣṭamānamantareṇa na saṃbhavati bhogasyāpi kriyātvāt tatkartṛtvenāpyātmasiddhiriti bhāvaḥ. samīhiteti. abhīṣṭetyarthaḥ. atra codayati.

(66A)
na vinā dṛṣṭasamvādamanumānasya mānatā

iha hi dhūmenānumito 'gnirāsīdatā pratyakṣīkriyata iti tasyānumānasya pramāṇāntarsaṃvādo dṛśyate. ata eva tasya prāmānyam. cakramūrdhādau dhūmāderiva sādhyavyabhīcārādarśanāt tataścātrāpyanubhavātmano jñānasyaiva darśanād jñātṛjñānayorākārabhedānupalambhād bhogād bhoktranumānasyāpi vyabhicāraśaṅkyā pramāṇatvābhāvānna bhokturjñānavyatiriktasyātmanaḥ siddhiriti saugatāḥ. yadāhuḥ ekamevedaṁ saṃvidrūpaṁ harṣaviṣādādyanekākāravivartaṁ paśyāmaḥ. tatra yatheṣṭam saṁjñāḥ kriyantāmiti. tadayuktamityāha.

(66B)

dṛṣṭasya kena saṃvādo yena tasyāsti mānatā

ayamabhiprāyaḥ. bhogasya viṣayasaṁvedanātmano 'nubhavasya bāhyaviṣayāsannidhane 'pi suṣuptyādāvāntaradehasparśamātraviṣayatvena sthiratayaiva bhāsamānatvāt sthiratvena svasaṁvedanapratyakṣasiddho grāhakarūpo ātmetyuktaṁ na ca jñānasya kṣaṇikasya svātmani kriyāvirodhenasthairyādhyāropo yuktaḥ. yadapyuktaṁ akṣaṇikasya kramayaugapadyābhyāmarthakriyāvirodhāt yatsat tatsarvaṁ kṣaṇikamiti. tadapi na. akṣaṇikasyaiva maṇyādeḥ krameṇa ghaṭādīn bhāvānavabhāsayato yugapañcaikagṛhagatāṁstāṁstānarthān prakāśayato 'nubhavasiddhatvāt. kṣaṇikasya cotpattikāla eva naśyato 'nekakṣaṇanirvartyakriyānuṣṭānākṣamatvādityādi vistareṇa śrīmanmataṅgavṛttyādāvācāryaiḥ sādhitamiti. tataścātmanaḥ svasaṁvedanasiddhatve' pyanumeyatvamabhyupagamyocyate.

(67A)

neha pramāṇasaṁvādaḥ pratyakṣasya pramāṇataḥ

nātra pramāṇasya pramāṇāntarasaṁvādāpekṣā. pratyakṣasya pramāṇāntarasaṃvādābhāve 'pyanadhigataviṣayajñānajanakatvena prāmāṇyāt. tadāhuḥ anadhigatārthagantṛ pramāṇaṁ iti. kathaṁ punaścakramūrdhādau vyabhicāro 'ta āha.

(67B)

anvayavyatirekābhyāṁ vyabhicāranirākṛtiḥ

yasya dhūmāderyenā 'vinābhāvalakṣaṇaḥ saṃbandho' nvayavyatirekābhyāṁ niścitaḥ na tasya tatra vyabhicāro dṛśyate. suvivecitasya dhūmasyā 'gnāviva. cakramū-rdhādijanyasya tu svarūpāvivekena dhūmatvabhrāntiḥ. tataścātrāpi kriyāyāḥ sarvatra kartṛpūrvakatvadarśanād bhogakriyayā bhoktrā 'numīyate. bhavadbhirapi svadehe buddhipūrvakatvena siddhāt kāryādivyavahārāt paraśarīre buddhiḥ pramāṇāntarasaṃvādaṁ vinā 'pyanumānenā' numīyate ityāha.

(68A)

dehadharmasya mānatve kāraṇaṁ buddhiriṣyate

dehadharmasya ceṣṭādyātmano mānatve hetutve sati tena paraśarīre taddheturbuddhiḥ sādhyate ityarthaḥ. yadāhuḥ buddhipūrvāṁ kriyāṁ dṛṣṭvā svadehe 'nyatra tadgrahāt. jñyate dhīḥ iti. ataśca rūpādidarśanānyathānupapattyā cakṣurādīndriyavad bhogānyathānupapattyā bhoktṛsiddirityabhiprāyeṇāha.

(68B-69Aa)

asmāt sāmānyato dṛṣṭādanyasyāpi pramāṇatā
anumānasya saṃsiddhā

yaduktaṁ cārvākaiḥ. astu bhoktā. sa tu paridṛśyamānapṛthivyādicaturbhūtavikārasamāhārātmakaḥ kāya eva. tasyaiva pariṇāmaviśeṣena kiṇvādidravyavikāreṇa madaśaktyabhivyaktavaccaitanyābhivyaktiḥ. prāṇādivāyubalena bhogādikriyādarśanācca. na tu tato 'nyaḥ. tasya pratyakṣenādarśanāt.
yadāhuḥ. dṛṣṭe saṁbhavatyadṛṣṭaparikalpanā na nyāyyā. iti. tadapi nirākṛtamityāha.

(69Ab-70A)

kāraṇādata eva hi
cetano buddhibodhasya bhoktā mānasamarthitaḥ
pṛthivyādisamāhāro bhavatviti na yuktimat

ayamabhiprāyaḥ. yataḥ śarīrasyāpyantaḥ śūlādyātmanā bahiśca mṛdukarkaśādinā sparśena bhogyatvadarśanād ghaṭādivaccetanatvaṁ na yuktam. tatastasyāpi bhoktṛtvenā' tmā siddha iti cetanatvaṁ cāsya na pramāṇopapannamityāha.

(70B)

caitanyam hi tvayā tasya kena mānena niścitam

nanu śuklaśoṇitātmakadehārambhakabhūtasadbhāva eva caitanyadarśanāt tadabhāve cā 'darśanād dehātmakameva caitanyamata āha.

(71Aa)

sati bhāve 'pyanaikāntaḥ

śavaśarīre garbhādau vā dehātmakabhūtasadbhāve 'pi caitanyā 'darśanānna dehātmakaṁ caitanyaṁ tataśca śarīrā' tmavādo na pramāṇopapanna ityaha.

(71Ab)

tasmād vāyasavāśitam

bhogyatvāccāsyā 'cetanatvamityāha.

(71B-72A)

anabhivyaktacaitanyā dṛṣṭā bhogyā guḍādayaḥ
jīvacchāyopabhogyatvādastu tulyo guḍādibhiḥ

guḍādayo hi jīvasyā 'tmanaśchāyayā 'nubhavātmanā saṃvidā bhogyatvena grāhyatayā viṣayīkriyamāṇāḥ kadācidapyabhivyaktacetanā na dṛṣṭāḥ. tataḥ kāyā 'tmāpi bhūtasamāhāraḥ proktavadgrāhyatvena bhogyatayā viṣayīkaraṇādacetana eveti na tasya bhoktṛtvamupapadyate. kiñca dehasyaiva cetanatve tasyā 'sakṛtpariṇāmena vināśād bālyāvāsthā 'nubhūtaṁ vṛddhāvasthāyaṁ smaryamāṇām nopapadyata ityādi vistareṇa nirākṛto 'yam pakṣo 'smābhiḥ śrīmanmṛgendravṛttidīpikāyām. nanu śarīravyatiriktānāmiṇ-driyāṇāmeva bhoktṛtvamastu. nānyasyetindriyacaitaṅi-kāḥtadayuktamityāha.

(72B-73A)

bhogyatvakaraṇatvābhyāmindriyāṇāṁ viniścitam
acaitanyamato bhoktā puruṣaścitsvabhāvakaḥ

uktavadindriyāṇāmapi bhogārthatayā bhogyatvāt karaṇ-atvācchastrādivadacetanatvamanivāryamevāto naiṣāṁ kartṛtvaṁ api tu citsvabhāvasyātmana eva. tasyaiva hi sarvānyakārakapravṛttinivṛttihetutvena kartṛtvaṁ yuktaṁ. yadāhuḥ pravṛttau ca nivṛttau ca kārakāṇāṁ ya īśvaraḥ. apravṛttaḥ pravṛttau vā sa kartā nāma kāraka iti.

(73B)

bhokturbhogaścitervyaktirbhogyacchāyānurañjitā

bhogyāyā buddheḥ sukhādirūpāyāśchāyayā ākāreṇānurāñjitā

caitanyavyaktireva bhokturbhogaḥ. yaduktaṁ śrīmatsvāyambhuve bhogo 'sya vedanā puṃsaḥ sukhaduḥkhādilakṣanā iti. tadānīṁ ca.

(74A)

acittaścitisaṃbandhād bhogyamābhāti cetanam

acetanamapi buddhyātmakaṁ bhogyaṁ tasyātmanaś caitanyasaṃśleṣāccetanavadābhāsate. taduktaṁ sāṁkhyairapi acetanaṁ cetanāvadiva liṅgam iti. evam ca.

(74B-75A)

bhogyadvārena pāśānāṁ paśunāṁ ca parasparam
cetanācetanacchāyānuṣaṅgo bhāsate bhṛśam

bhogyaṁ hi vastu cittādhiṣṭhitaṁ buddhīndriyabṛndamātmano viṣayatvenopasthāpayati. tacca buddhyā' dhyavasitaṁ puruṣo gṛhṇāti. yadāhuḥ buddhyādhyavasitamarthaṁ puruṣaścetayati iti. tataśca prakāścarūpatvādārśasthānīyena bhogākhyena buddhibodhātmanā dvāreṇātmanānāṁ bhoktṛṇāṁ pāśānāṁ ca viṣayarūpeṇa pariṇatānāṁ bhogyānāṁ cetanācetanarūpayośchāyayoḥ pratibimbitayorākāranuṣaṅgaḥ saṃśleṣamātraṁ bhṛśamatyarthamekākāratayā bhāsate. ata evātrānātmādau ātmādibhramaḥ saṃsāriṇām. tadvivekajñāne tu teṣām prakṛtilaya ityuktam. sa eva ca sāṁkhyānāṁ mokṣaḥ ataśca.

(75B)

bhogye bhogaḥ prabhośchāyā yathā candramaso jale

prabhorvyāpakasyātmanaḥ sa eva bhogyaviṣayo bhogaḥ. yā tadadhyavasāyātmani buddhibodhe candramasa iva jale chāyāviśiṣtā caitanyābhivyaktiḥ candrabimbasya jaḍatvāt sthūlatvācca viśiṣtasvarūpābhivyaktimātra evātra dṛṣṭāntatvam. ato bhoktṛtvāccetanasya puruṣasyaiva kartṛtvaṁ nācetanānāṁ bhogyānāṁ buddhyādināmiti mantavyam. nanu kriyāveśo hi kartṛvam. sa yadi puṃsaḥ syāt pariṇāmitā bhavet. puruṣo hi nirvikāraḥ tato nāsya kartṛtvam. kintu prakṛtereva sā hi vivekajñānāt pūrvaṁ mahadādirūpeṇa bhogyatayā tasyātmānaṁ darśayatīti saṃsāra ityucyate. tatsaṃbhave tu tasmānnivartamāna muktiśabdābhidheyeti sāṁkhyāḥ. yaduktaṁ taiḥ. raṅgasya darśayitvā nivartate nartakī yathā raṅgāt. puruṣasya tathātmānaṁ prakāśya vinivartate prakṛtiḥ iti. ata āha.

(76A-76B)

pariṇāmabhayāt puṃsi bhoge cānīpsite sati
aviśeṣo durāpohaḥ prasakto bhoktṛmuktayoḥ

ayamabhiprāyaḥ. nātra kriyāveśaḥ kartṛtvam. api tu kriyāyāṁ śaktatvameva. tathāhi ayaskāntasannidhānādaya ivātmanaḥ sannidheḥ śarīrādereva spandādirūpaḥ kriyāveśo dṛśyate. tataśca buddhyādivisayīkaraṇarūpe bhoge puṃso na pariṇāmaprasaṅgaḥ. kintu tatparatvena tadviṣayīkaraṇameva. bhavatpakṣe tu puṃso nirmalatvena tatparatve' pyanabhyupagamyamāne bhoktṛmuktayoraviśeṣo durnivāraḥ prasajyate. ubhayorapyanapekṣatvena tulyatvāt. nanu parārthapravṛtta prakṛtireva tadarthaṁ pravartata ityuktam. yadāhuḥ vatsavivṛddhiṅimittaṁ kṣīrasya. yathā pravṛttirajñasya. puruṣavimokṣanimittaṁ tathā pravṛttiḥ pradhānasyeti. ata āha.

(77A)

pumarthāya ca pāśānāṁ pravṛttirvinivāritā

ayamabhiprāyaḥ acetanatvādeva pradhānasya puruṣam prati pravṛttirna yuktā. kṣīrāderapi cetanagavādyadhiṣṭitasyaiva pravṛttidṛṣṭaiḥ. vāyujalādīnāmapi pakṣīkṛtatvācca tatpravṛttyabhyupagame 'py na nirapekṣaṁ prati pravṛttiryuktā. nirapekṣaṁ prati pravṛttau va muktasyāpi pravartate. tataśca baddhātmani sābhilāṣatve bhogārthaṁ samudyogādātmani vikāre cā 'nabhyupagamyamāne tasmin bhogo 'pi na yuktimānityāha.

(77B)

bhoktaryavikṛte bhogo muktavannopapadyate

nanvaviveka eva pradhānapravṛtterhetuḥ. prakṛtipuruṣavivekajñāne tu taṁ pratyuparatādhikāratvānna pravartate. ato na baddhamuktayoraviśeṣaḥ yadāhuḥ prakṛteḥ sukumārataraṁ na kiñcidastīti me matirbhavati yā dṛṣṭāsmīti punar darśanamupaita puruṣasya iti. tadayuktaṁ. bhavatpakṣe puṃso nirmalatvenāvivekāyogāt. nirhetuke cāviveke sarvadā vivekābhāvaprasaṅgācca. tasmādavivekānyathānupapattyāpi tasya samalatvasarāgatādyadhyupagantavyamiti vakṣyāmaḥ. yadyevamātmanaḥ samalatvenājñasvabhāvatve śarīrādiyogena jñātṛtaya vikāre cābhyupagamyamāne svabhāvāntarayogād-anityatvaprasaṅga iti paramatmāśaṅkate.

(78Aa)

vikāritvādanityaścet

bhokteti śeṣaḥ. pariharati.

(78Ab)

māyāsādhyaṁ na manyate

māyayā svakāryaiḥ sūkṣmabāhyaśarīradvāreṇa kriyamāṇaṁ viśeṣaṁ na jānīte bhavāniti śeṣaḥ. tato nānityatvādidoṣa ityabhiprāyaḥ. kathamityata āhaḥ.

(78B)

svarūpavyaktilābhācca na vikāro na nāśitā

nāsmābhirnaiyāyikādivajjaḍarūpa evā 'tmā iṣyate. api tu jñasvabhāva eva. sa tu tasya svabhāvaḥ śarīrādiyogaṁ vinā' nabhivyakteranādinā kenā 'pi pratibaddho 'vasīyate. sa ca mala eveti vakṣyāmaḥ. tataśca māyayā kalādibhiḥ svakāryamalavyudāse naikadeśasvarūpavyaktirevātmanaḥ kriyate. malaparipāke tu dīkṣākhyayā Śivaśaktyā sarvaviṣayo' bhivyajyate. tato nāsya vikāro vināśitā ceti. asya ca.

(79A)

bhogyopadhānarāgaśca svacchatvānnoktakāraṇāt

ato bhogyaviṣayopadhānajanito rāgo 'pi sukhadu-ḥkhamohākāraḥ prakāśo 'sya sphaṭikasyeva svacchatvāt prakāśarūpatvāt na tu pūrvoktāt pariṇāmākhyāt kāraṇāt. sa ca viṣayoparāgo 'pyasya tatparatayā tadviṣayīkaraṇam. evetyuktam. tato bhogyasya śarīrasyāsakṛtpariṇāme 'pi bhokturna pariṇāma ityāha.

(79B-80A)

śarīrapariṇame na pariṇāmī na pudgalaḥ
sa yato' cetano bhogyo buddhivat pariṇāmataḥ

tasyāpi pariṇāmābhyupagame buddhyādivadbhogyatvam-acetanatvaṁ ca syādityarthaḥ. tatra paramatamupanyasya dūṣayati.

(80B-81A)

caitanyaṁ hi guṇo jñānaṁ samavāyo 'tha tena vā
svarūpaṁ puruṣasyeti nānyadasya na yuktimat

evaṁ hi naiyāyikādayo manyante. jaḍasvabhāva evā 'tmā tasya manaḥ saṁyogād guṇatayā jñānaṁ samavetamutpadyate. tadeva ca tasya caitanyaṁ nānyajjñasvabhāvatvamiti. tadayuktam. jaḍatve tasya ghaṭādvajjñānasamavāyāyogāditi. nanvatra niyāmakaṁ karmādṛṣṭākhyamasti. yatkarmasa-mānādhikaraṇe puruṣa eva jñānaṁ samavetamutpadyate. nānyatra tadvyadhikaraṇe ghaṭādāviti. ata āha.

(81B-82A)

ajñe naryeva vijñānaṁ nānyatreti niyāmakam
karmā 'pi nopapannaṁ tu tadanyatra sthitaṁ yataḥ

karmaṇaḥ kṛṣyāderiva prakṛtisaṃskāratvameva nātmasaṁskāratvaṁ vikāritvaprasaṅgādityuktam. tatastadapi nātra niyāmakaṁ bhavitumarhati. tataścaitanyasam-avāyaccitsvabhāva evātmā siddha ityāha.

(82B-83A)

moho mohasvabhāvebhyo yadvannārthāntaraṁ budhāḥ
caitanyebhyaḥ caitanyebhyaḥ
padārthebhayastadvannārthāntaraṁ citiḥ

caitanyātmano jñānasyātmadharmatvād dharmanāśe dharmiṇo 'pi tadavyatirekānnāśaḥ prasajyata iti sarvadā cetanasvabhāva evātmabhyupagantavyaḥ. tasya ca malāvṛtatvānmanobuddhyādayastadabhivyañjakatayā siddhā ityuktam. asya ca bhogakriyāyāmupakārakatayā sahakāri-bhūtaṁ prayoktṛkaraṇarañjakarūpaṁ kalāvidyārāgākhyaṁ kañcukatrayaṁ prakṛtisādhanāt paścādabhidhāsyate ityāha.

(83B-84A)

prayoktṛkaraṇaṁ bhoge rañjakaṁ copari trayam
asya bhogakriyākartuḥ prakṛterupadekṣyate

itthaṁ prasaṅgād bhoktāraṁ prasādhya prakṛte buddherevāhaṅkārasyotpattirityāha.

(84B-85A)

buddheḥ skandho 'paro bhinno yo'haṅkāramajījanat
janitāro guṇā yena dṛṣṭāstatpratibhādiṣu

yena kāraṇena tasyā buddheḥ pratibhādiṣu vṛttiṣu proktena nayena parasparābhibhavenāśrayānmithunī bhāvācca kāryasyotpādayitāro guṇāḥ dṛṣṭāḥ. yaduktaṁ sāṁkhyaiḥ anyonyābhibhavāśrayajananamithunapravṛttayaśca guṇāḥ iti tena buddherevādhyavasāyahetoḥ skandhādanyo bhāgo guṇasaṁpṛkto 'haṅkāramajījanat. tataśca na hyekaṁ janakamiti nyāyenānyonyasaṃpṛktā eva guṇā janakāstathaiva ca sarveṣu padārtheṣu vartane. sāttvikādivyavahārastu teṣāṁ sāttvikdibāhulyāditi bhāvaḥ. sākṣādguṇakāryatvādeva cāsyāṁ guṇānvayo ghaṭādiṣu mṛdakārānvayavadityāha.

(86B-86A)

prathamā vikṛtiḥ sā 'to guṇānāṁ tatra yujyate
udbhāvabhibhavābhyāṁ tu niyamena vyavasthitiḥ

guṇa hi tasyāṁ niyamena paramparābhibhavena bhavantaḥ siddhyādijanakā ityuktam. yadyevamahaṅkārasyāpi guṇānvayād guṇebhya evotpattirastu ata āha.

(86B-87A)

ahaṅkāre 'pyayaṁ nyāya iti mā jalpa paṇḍita
anyonyavikṛtitvāt tanmātrāsvapyanuṣajyate

ahaṅkārādibhūtāntānāṁ sarveṣāmapyanyonyavikṛtitvāt proktavatparamparayā guṇavikāratvānna kevalamahaṅkāra eva tanmātrāsvapi apiśabdādindriyavarge bhūtavarge ca guṇānvayo 'nuṣajyata eva. ghaṭakapālādiṣu mṛdākārānvayavat. na tu sarveṣām sākṣād guṇebhya evotpattirityadoṣaḥ. atha ke te guṇāḥ kairvyāpāraiśca teṣām siddhir ityata āha.

(87B-88A)

sattvaṁ rajastamaśceti kāraṇāni dhiyo guṇāḥ
prakhyāvyāpāraniyamaiḥ puṃyogaṁ ye vitenire

proktavadbuddhyādidvāreṇa bhāvapratyayādirūpaṁ puruṣabhogyam vastu ye sargādau cakrarutpāditavantaḥ adhunāpi kurvate te buddherapi kāraṇam guṇā iti. ete ca parasparāviyogādekameva tattvam. yacchrūyate. trayo guṇāstathāpyekaṁ tattvam tadaviyogataḥ. iti. tato buddhikāraṇatayā prakāśavṛttiniyamākhyairvyāpāraiḥ sattvādinaṁ siddhiḥ. ete ca prādhānyāt pradarśitāḥ. anyeṣāmapi stairyadhairyādīnāṁ śauryakrauryādīnāmaratimāndyādīnāṁ guṇakāryāṇāmāgameṣu śravaṇāt. nanu guṇā eva pradhānākhyā nityatvena sthitā. iti. sāṃkhyāḥ tadayuktamityāha.

(88B-89A)

acaitanye 'pyanekatvasaṃkhyāsaṃbandhahetutaḥ
teṣāṁ kāraṇapūrvatvamiṣṭaṁ buddhighaṭādivat

yata eṣāmanekatvasaṁkhyāsaṁbandhādanekatvaṁ tato' nekatvādacetanatvācca ghaṭādivat kāryatvasiddhiḥ. kim teṣāmupādānamityata āha.

(89B-90A)

upādānaṁ guṇānāṁ yat prakṛtiḥ sābhidhīyate
avibhāgasthitā yasyāṁ nirgacchanti śiveritaḥ

yasyāṁ sūkṣmatvenāvibhāgena sthitā guṇāḥ śivapreraṇena svasvapravṛttivibhāgaiḥ sthūlāḥ abhivyajyante sā prakṛtiḥ. śiveriteti cācetanatvānnāsyāḥ svātantryeṇa pravṛttiriti darśayati. asyāśca pratipuruṣaṁ sūkṣmadehavartitvenānekatvāt kāryatvamiti vakṣyāmaḥ. atha puruṣasya kalādipañcakañcukayuktasya bhoktṛtvena puṁstvamalayogād dīkṣāyāṁ tacchuddhyarthaṁ prakṛtitattvādūrdhvamāgameṣu paṭhe satyapi tasya vyāpakatvāccetanatvena bhoktṛtvāccādhvarūpatvaṁ bhogasādhanatvaṁ ca na saṃbhavatīti tamupekṣya tasyaiva rañjakatvena prāguktaṁ rāgatattvaṁ sādhayitumāha.

(90B-91A)

bhogyānubhavamāsādya bhogye śaktiḥ pravartate
tatsiddhyarthaṁ tatastasya rāgo bhogānurañjakaḥ

iha hi saṁsārāvasthāyāṁ puruṣasya bhogyaṁ dṛṣṭvā tasmin saktiḥ pravartate. sā ca nāheturutpadyate. muktyavasthāyāmapi prasaṅgāt. atastasya puṃsastasyāḥ sakteḥ siddhyarthaṁ bhogābhilāṣajanako rāgo 'bhyupagantavyaḥ. atra parābhiprāyaḥ.

(91B-92A)

sattvaṁ rajastamo yuktaṁ viṣayeṣvanurañjakam
buddhāvabhyuditaṁ puṁsastasmādanyo nirarthakaḥ

pariharati.

(92B-93A)

tanmatāvuditaṁ bhogyaṁ tasmin yo 'syānurañjakaḥ
sa rāgo 'nyaḥ pramantavyo rūpe 'pyetaddhi dūṣaṇam

sāttvikādibhogasādhanaviṣayākārādhyavasāyadvāreṇa buddhāvuditasya sukhaduḥkhamoharūpeṇa pariṇatasya sattvādiguṇatrayasyaiva sākṣādbhogyatvāt tasminnapi bhogye yaḥ puṁso 'bhilāṣajanakaḥ sa tasmādviṣayaguṇādirūpeṇa buddhāvuditātattvādiguṇatrayādbhogyarūpādanyo grāhakagato rāgo mantavyaḥ. bhogyasyaivā 'bhilāṣajanakatve vītarāgabhāvaprasaṅga iti bhāvaḥ. taduktam tattvasaṁgrahe bhogyaviśeṣa rāge nahi kaścidvītarāgaḥ syāt iti. yadyevamavairāgyalakṣaṇo buddhidharma eva rāgo 'stvata āha. rūpe 'pyetaddhi dūṣaṇamiti. ayamabhiprāyaḥ. avairāgyalakṣaṇasya rūpasya tāvadvāsanārūpatvānna kāryakaratvam. vāsanāvasthāyāmapi kāryakaratve buddheranantavāsanāyogena puṁso yugapadviruddhā 'nantapratipattivaiśasaprasaṅgāt.

pratyayātmanā sthūlarūpeṇa bhogyadaśāmāpannena tasmin rāge 'bhyupagamyamāne 'pi prāgvadvitārāgābhāvaprasaṅga iti tayoranyo rago 'bhyupagantavya iti. karmaiva rañjakamastviti cenna. tasya kṛsyādivatphalajanana eva caritārthatvāt kāryāntarahetutve pramāṇābhāvāt anekatatvaparikalpanābhāvaprasaṅgācca. atha vidyāsiddhiḥ.

(93B-94A)

karaṇaṁ na vinā kartuḥ kṛtiḥ karmaṇi dṛśyate
ato 'sti karaṇaṁ vidyā buddhibodhavivecinī

proktavadindriyāṇāṁ viṣayopasthāpakatvenopayogāt. tasmin buddhibodhākhye karmaṇi grāhye grahaṇakriyānāṁ puṁsaḥ kenāpi karaṇena bhavitavyaṁ. yattatkaraṇam sā vidyeti. atra paraḥ.

(94B-95A)

pradīpavanmatistasya svaparātmaprakāśikā
vidyate karaṇam puṁso vidyayā kiṁ kariṣyati

buddheḥ prakāśarūpatvāt pradīpavadviṣayākāraṁ svātmānamapi prakāśayatīti na karaṇāntarasiddhiḥ. pariharati.

(95B-96A)

pradīpaḥ karaṇaṁ puṁsaḥ staṁbhādyart hopalabdhiṣu
dīpopalabdhau cakṣuśca buddhāvapyevamiṣyatām

buddherapi grāhyatvena karmatvāt karaṇāpekṣā 'stīty-uktamiti bhāvaḥ. uktam ca tattvasaṁgrahe 'ravivat prakāśarūpo yadi nāmamahāṁstathāpi karmatvāt. karaṇāntarasāpekṣaḥ śakto grāhayitumātmānam iti. etad eva darśayati.

(96B-97A)

traiguṇyāt sā vivekena śaktā darśayituṁ nahi
viṣayākāramātmānamaviviktā yataḥ svayam

(97B-98A)

vidyā guṇaparā vedyaṁ viviktā' to vivekataḥ
śaktā darśayituṁ puṁso nā 'tra kāryo 'timatsaraḥ

buddhestriguṇātmakatvena bhogyākāravivekāt karmatayā na svātmaprakāśatvaṁ pradīpādivat. vidyā tu tadatītatvena bhogyākārād viviktā satī puṁso vedyaṁ karaṇāntaranirapekṣā prakāśayatyeveti. atha kalāyā vyāpāraḥ kathyate.

(98B-99A)

karmādikārakānīkaprayoktā bhogasiddhaye
svatantraḥ puruṣaḥ kartā kalā tasya prayojikā

bhoktṛtvena bhogārthaṁ buddhyādikārakavrātaprayoktṛtvāt kartā puruṣa ityuktam. pravṛttau ca nivṛttau ca kārakāṇām ya īśvaraḥ apravṛttaḥ pravṛttau vā sa kartā nāma kārakaḥ iti. tasya ca bhogakriyāyāṁ vakṣyamāṇavat sāmarthyopodbalena prayojikā kalā śāstreṣūcyate.nanvakartaiva puruṣa iti sāṅkhyāḥ. tadyuktaṁ ityāha.

(99B-100A)

akartṛtvā 'bhyupagame bhoktṛśabdo nirarthakaḥ
upādānapravṛtteśca niṣphalatvam prasajyate

bhogasyā 'pi kriyātvādhoktṛtvenaiva puṁsaḥ kartṛtvaṁ siddhyati. tasminnakartaryabhyupagamyamāne tadbhogārthaṁ pradhānasyā 'pi pravṛttirniṣphalā syāt. akartari karaṇādisaṁbandhasya nirarthakatvāt. kiñca.

(100B-101A)

kartṛmat karmadevādi kriyāsādhanabhāvataḥ
vāsyādivadataḥ kartā parijñeyo vibhuh pumān

avibhutve hyātmano gaganādivadamūrtātvād deśāntaranayanā 'saṁbhavena dākṣiṇātyādeḥ kaśmīrādau dṛśyamāno deśāntaraphalabhogo 'nupapanna iti tadanyathā 'nupataptyā' tma vyāpako'bhyupagantavyah. iti. uktaṁ ca śrīmatparākhyādau kartṛśaktiṁ vyanaktyasya kalā 'syātaḥ prayojikā. tataḥ kalāsamāyukto bhoge 'ṇuḥ kartṛkārakaḥ iti. asya kartuḥ puṁsaḥ kartṛśaktiḥ śakterekatvājjñākriyā-śaktirvakṣyamāṇavat malāvṛtatvenārtheṣu na pravartata iti pradīpavat prakāśarūpā kalaikadeśe malavidāraṇena tāmabhivyanakti prakāśayati. tataḥā prayojikā hetuḥ kartrī bhaṇyate. sa cāṇuḥ puruṣastaya 'tyantāvivekena bhāsamāno bhogakriyāyāṁ kartṛkārakamucyate. sa hi bhoktṛtvāt kartā kalā tu tatprayojikātvāt kārakamiti. taduktaṁ śrīmanmṛgendre ityetadubhayam viprasaṁbhūyā 'nanyavat sthitaṁ bhogakriyāvidhau jantornirjaguḥ kartṛkārakamiti. anyathā hi.

(101B-102A)

vyaktikartranapekṣasya kartṛbhāve samīhite
ātmanaḥ prākkalāyogāt prasaktā sarvakartṛtā

(102B-103A)

sarvakartṛtvasaṁbandhāt sarvajñaḥ parameśavat
sarvajñatvādayuktā 'sya svātmaduḥkhāya kartṛtā

ātmano hi nirmalatvena kalānapekṣasyaiva kartṛtve' bhyupagamyamāne śivavat kalādipāśātmakaśarīrasaṃbandhaṁ vinaiva sarvakartṛtvaṁ ajñātasya karaṇāsambhavena sarvajñatvaṁ ca bhavet. niravāraṇatvena śivenā 'nadhiṣṭhitasya svatantrasyā 'sya svātmana eva duḥkhāya śarīrādikartṛtvaṁ na yujyate. ato 'sya sukhotpādādau pāratantryadarśanād baddhatvaṁ samalatvaṁ ca niścīyate. tata eva cā' syāsarvakartṛtvaṁasarvajñatvaṁ ca saṁsārāvasthāyām dṛśyate. tato malāvṛtatvādasya bhoge viṣaye kiñcijjñatva-kartṛtvayorapi kalānugrahāpekṣā siddhetyāha

(103B-104A)

na cāsya sarvakartṛtvaṁ baddhatvād govṛṣādivat
kalānugrahasāpekṣā bhoge tenā 'sya kartṛtā

itthaṁ kalāṁ prasāddhya tasyā eva vidyārāgāvyaktānām-udbhava ityāha.

(104B-105A)

skandho 'paraḥ kalāyāstu yasmādetāḥ prajajñire
vidyārāgaprakṛtayo yugmāyugmakrameṇa tu

yugmakrameṇa rāgavidye sahaiva jāyete. avyaktaṁ tu pṛthagayugmakrameṇetyarthaḥ. uktaṁ ca śrīmadraurave kalātattvādrāgavidye dve tattve saṁbabhūvatuḥ. avyaktaṁ ca iti. atra karmaphalabhogasya kāla' vacchedaṁ bhoktṛniyamaṁ ca vinā 'nutpatteḥ kālaniyatyākhyaṁ tattva- dvayāmāgameṣu śrūyamāṇamarthasiddhatvādācāryeṇā' nupattam. tathāhi kṛṣyādivat karmaphalānāṁ rājaniyamā' bhāve dasyubhirapahāradarśaṇād. jyotiṣṭomādikarmap-halānāmapi bhoktṛpratiniyāmakena kenā 'pi bhāvyamiti tanniyāmakatvena niyatiḥ sidhhā. karmaṇo niyāmak-atvamastīti cettanna. tasya phalajanana eva caritārthatvād-ityuktam. īśvaraśakterapi tattvāntaravyavadhānenaiva bhogaviṣaye kāryakaratvam. anyathā sarvatattvābhāvap-rasaṅgāt. kiñca cirakṣiprādipratyayadvārena ciraṁ bhuṅkte ityādibhogyādyavacchedakatvena kālaḥ siddhaḥ. sa ca na naiyāyikādyabhyupagatavannityo bhavitumarhati, bhūtādir-upatvenānekatvādacetanatvācca. taduktạm śrīmanmṛgendre truṭyādipratyayasyārthaḥ kālo māyāsamudbhavaḥ. kạlyannā samutthānānniyatyā niyataṁ paśuṁ iti. ittham sūkṣmadehātmikāṁ tattvasaṁhatimuktavā tasyāḥ pratipuruṣam niyatatvamāha.

(105B-106A)

vasudhādikalāprāntā bhogasādhanasaṃhatiḥ
niyatā pratibhoktāraṁ parijñeya manīṣbhiḥ

taduktaṁ tattvasaṁgrahe. vasudhādyastattvaguṇaḥ pratipumniyataḥ kalānto 'yam. paryaṭati karmavaśato bhuvanajadeheṣvayaṁ ca sarveṣu iti. ekatve sukṣmadehasya sarveṣāṁ dṛśyamānabhogabhedo na yukta ityahạ.

(106B)

anyathā hi sukhādīnāṁ dṛṣṭo bhedo na yujyate

naṇvekatve 'pi sūkṣmadehasya karmabhedādeva tatphalabhogabhedo bhaviṣyatīti cet tadayuktamityāna

(107A)

yokṣyate karmaṇo bhedāt tadbhedo yadi yokṣyate

karmabhedādeva bhogabhedaḥ siddhyati. siddhe ca bhogabhede karmabhedo 'numīyata itītaretarāśrayadoṣaḥ prasakta ityarthaḥ. nanu kartṛbhedādeva siddhaḥ karmabhedaḥ karmabhedācca bhogabheda iti nānyonyāśrayadoṣaḥ. ata āha

(107B-108A)

saṃbandhādyugapat sā tu kurvantī karmakartṛbhiḥ
kathaṁ bhinnāni karmāni kartṛbhedāt kariṣyati

malāvṛtatvenā 'tmanāṁ kalādisūkṣmadehādisaṁbandhaṁ vinā karmakartṛtvā 'nupapatteḥ. yugapatsarvakartṛsaṁbandhena karma kurvāṇā sā sūkṣmadeharūpā tattvasaṁhatirekarūpā kathaṁ bhinnāni vicitrāṇi karmāṇi karoti naivetyarthaḥ. nanu pratipuruṣaṁ cikīrṣābhedātkarmabheda iti cettanna. cikīrṣāyāśca sūkṣmadehasaṁbandhādevotpatteḥ. tasyāścaikatvāccikīrṣābhedo' pyanupapanna iti paridṛśyamānabhogabhedānyathā' nupapattyā pratipuruṣaṁ sukṣmadehabhedo 'vaśyamabhyupagantavyaḥ. nanvātmabhede hi sūkṣmadehabhedo yuktaḥ. sa eva tāvadeka iti vedāntavidastatrā 'ha.

(108B)

ātmanāmapyanekatvamata eva pratīyate

ekatve hyātmanaḥ sukhaduḥkhādivaicitryaṁ janmamaraṇavaicitryaṁ cānupapannamiti bhogavaicitryādeva' tmanānātvasiddhiḥ. eṣa cādvaitanirāso 'smābhirmṛgendravṛttidīpikāyāṁ vistareṇa darśitaḥ. atha kimiyaṁ sūkṣmadeharūpā tattvasaṁhatirātmavad vyāpikā. āhosvidavyāpiketyata āha.

(109A)

tasyāścāvibhutā siddhā yugapad vṛttyasaṁbhavāt

jñānakriyābhivyaktilakṣaṇasya tatkāryasya sarvatra yugapadanutpatteśtasyāścāvyāpakatvasiddhiḥ. nanu yatra sahakāriṇā karmaṇā phalārambheṇa nirdeśo bhavati tatraivāsāvātmanaścaitanyābhivyaktaye vikṣobhamabhivyañjanarūpaṁ karotīti tasmādevāsyāḥ sarvatra yugapatkāryānutpattirnāvyāpakatvāditi cet. tadapyayuktaṁ tasyāḥ kāryatvenā 'nityatvādghaṭādivad vyāpakatvā' siddherityabhiprāyeṇāha.

(109-110A)

karmanirdeśavikṣobhakaraṇatvaṁ ca nottaram
yugapad vṛttyanutpatteḥ sarvatra vibhutaiva na

atha kimiyamekadeśe caitanyābhivyaktiḥ sūkṣmadehavyāñjkasyā' vibhutvāt uta vyaṅgyasyā 'tmanaḥ ityata āha.

(110B-111A)

vikāritvādidharmyātmā virodhaśca śruteraṇau
avibhāu yugapaccittvavyakatikāle 'apyaṇurvibhuḥ

yadyavyāpaka ātmā syāt tadā deśāntaraphalopabhogo'pyanupapanna ityuktam. kiñca tasya muktyavasthāyāṁ śivavatsarvajñatvasarvakartṛkatvaśravaṇād vyāpakatvamavaśyamabhyupeyam. atha saṁsārāvasthāyām-avyāpakatvaṁ muktyavasthāyāṁ ca vyāpakatvaṁ tasyeṣyatẹ tadā pariṇāmitvācetanatvādidoṣaprasaṅgaḥ tato nityatvavyāpakatvādiśrutervirodhaḥ. taduktaṁ śrīmanmṛgendre caitanyaṁ dṛkkriyārūpaṁ tadastyātmani sarvadā sarvataśca yato muktau śrūyate sarvatomukhaṁ. iti. nāvyāpako na kṣaṇiko naiko nāpi jaḍātmakaḥ iti ca. itthaṁ sūkṣmadehātmikāmasādhāraṇatattvasṛṣṭimuktvā bhūvanātmikāṁ sādhāraṇatattvasṛṣṭimāha.

(111B)

tattvānāmapare skandhā bhogino ratibhūmayaḥ

sūkṣmadeharūpād bhogādanye vicitrabhuvanādyākārāstattvānāṁ bhogāḥ saṁsāriṇaḥ bhogasthānānītyarthaḥ. ataśca.

(112A)

tajjadehapraviṣṭa sā teṣāṁ tāsu phalāvahā

sūkṣmadehātmikā tattvasaṃhatirācārāpekṣayā tāsu bhogabhūmiṣu karmavaśāt tattadbhuvanajadeheṣu praviṣṭā satī puruṣasyaikadeśena jñānakriyāsāmarthyaṁśābhivyañjikā bhavati. taduktaṁ tattvasaṅgrahe paryaṭati karmavaśato bhuvanajadeheṣvayaṁ ca sarveṣu iti. śrimanmṛgendre 'pi. ityātivāhikamidaṁ vapurasya jantościtsaṅgacidgahanagarbhavivarti leśāt.naitāvatā 'lamiti bhauvanatattvapaṅktimādhāradehaviṣayā 'bhyudayāya vakṣye. iti. tāmeva bhuvanasṛṣṭiṁ saṃkṣepeṇa darśayati.

(112B-113A)

nirayādistu satyāntā kālahāṭakadeśikaiḥ
ādimadhyāntasaṃruddhā bhūteṣu sthānapaddhatiḥ

tatra kālaḥ. kālāgniḥ. hāṭakaḥ pātāḷādhipatiḥ. deśikaḥ samastaśāstropadeśakatvāllokācāryaḥ satyalokordhvasthitasya viṣṇulokasyāpyupari vartate. rudraloke vartamāno 'nantaśiṣyaḥ śrīkaṇṭhastasyaiva brahmāṇḍāntaradhikārāt taiḥ kālahāṭakadeśikaiḥ svasvabhuvanavartiṣvādimadhyānteṣvadhiṣṭhitā narakapātālabhūrādilokātmikā bhuvanapaddhatiḥ sthūleṣu brahmāṇḍāntarvartiṣu sthitā. tataśca.

(113B-114Ba)

śatarudravibhuśāpi saha pañcabhiraṣṭakaiḥ
mātrāsaṃbhūtabhūteṣu proktabhūtavidhātṛṣu
tanmātrā cittavargeṣu

tatra śatarudrāṇāṁ brahmāṇḍadhārakāṇāmadhiṣṭhātā vīrabhadraḥ pṛthivītattve prāguktasthūlapṛthivīkāraṇabhūte tanmātrā 'janye sūkṣmapṛthivītattve sthitaḥ. tathā sthūlajalādikāraṇabhūte tanmātrājanye eva sūkṣmajalādibhūtacatuṣṭaye. cittavargaśabdenāntaḥkaraṇānāmupādānāt tanmātrādyahaṅkārānte cā 'dhvani guhyātiguhyaguhyatarapavitrasthāṇvākhyāni pañcāṣṭakāni bhuvanānāṁ sthitāni. taduktam śrīmannandikeśvarakārikāsu brahmā stūlāni gataḥ sūkṣmādīnyādhāradehabhogyārthaṁ. rudraśataṁ kṣetrabhuvāṁ catvāriṁśacca sūkṣmabhūtāni. tanmātrā mano 'haṅkṛtibuddhirdeva guṇāmstu yogivarāḥ. vāmādyā guṇasāraṁ krodhāḥ prakṛtiṁ kalāṁ tu maṇḍalina iti. ata evā 'ha.

(114Bb-116B)

buddhau ca kramaśo nyaset
paiśācādyaṣṭakaṁ vidvān guṇatattve kṛtādikam
aprāptaguṇabhāve tu viśuddhe guṇamastake
vikāre prākṛte līnā vāmādisthānamālikā
krodheśvararudrāṇām purapaṅktiḥ pradhānagā

vāmadevādayastrayodaśa rudrāḥ krodheśādibhiraṣṭabhiḥ sahā pradhānā 'dhipairguṇamastakabhuvaneṣu sthitāḥ. prakṛteḥ sūkṣmarūpatvādbhuvanā 'dhāratvā 'yogādityāgamavidaḥ. tathā.

(117A)

maṇḍalāni tu vāmāṣṭau kalātattve sthitāni tu

rāgavidyāsahite kalātattve 'ṣṭāṣṭakrameṇāṣṭau bhuvanānāṁ maṇḍalāni sthitāni. taduktaṁ śrīmanmṛgendre rāgavidyāgarbhe kalāpade mahāpuracatuṣṣaṣṭhimaṇḍale maṇḍalādhipā iti. [V.13.143] kālaniyatyośca bhuvanadvayaṁ tatraivoktaṁ niyatau sthito niyataḥ kāle kalanaśaktimān. iti. eṣa ca bhuvanādhvā paddhatyādiṣu bahuśo dṛśyata iti nātra vistareṇa pradarśitaḥ. teṣu cā 'vāntarabhuvanasaṃkhyābhedaḥ keṣucit keṣāñcidantarbhāvādityavirodhaḥ. itthaṁ bhuvanātmikāmapi tattvasṛṣṭimuktvā proktasya kalādirūpasya jagataḥ paramopādānaṁ māyāṁ sādhayati.

(117B-118A)

jagadbījaṁ mahāmāyā janyaśaktiracetanā
tasyāḥ kalādisaṃbhūtirbhoginām bhogabhūtaye

mahatī cāsāvanekasrotorūpasvakāryavyāptermāyā ca mātyāsyaṁ praḷaye sarvamaśuddhaṁ jagaditi māyā. sā ca jagadbījaṁ jagataḥ kalādirūpasya pratipuruṣaṁ bhedenā' nekatvādbhuvanā 'dhāratvācca kāryarūpasya sarvasya sākṣāt paramparayā copādānam. ata eva janyaśaktiḥ sūkṣmarūpasvakāryaśaktisamāhārā 'tmikā satkāryavādā' bhyupagamena sarvakāryānāṁ śaktirūpeṇa tatrā 'vasthānāt. upādānatvādeva mṛdādivadacetanatā ca. tatastasyāḥ kalādibhogasādhanasaṁbhūtirityuktam. śaktisamāhārātmakatāmeva 'syāḥ prakaṭayati.

(118B-119A)

anekābhirvicitrābhiḥ śaktibhiḥ śaktimatyasau
vicitrā 'nantakāryāṇāṁ darśanāt saṁpratīyate

vicitrā 'nantakāryotpattidarśanād vicitrānantakāryaśaktisamāhārātmikā 'sau jñāyate. na tvasyā evā 'nekakāryajanikā' nekāḥ śaktayaḥ kalpyāḥ tasyāḥ svayaṁ śaktirūpatvācchakteśca śaktyantarakalpanā 'nupapatteḥ paramakāraṇatvādeva 'syā nityatvaṁ anyathā 'navasthāprasaṅgādityabhiprāyeṇā 'ha.

(119B-120A)

acidvatāmanekatvād vināśitvaṁ suniścitam
nā 'nekā sā tvato nityā māyā yadyapyacetanā

kiñca.

(120B-121A)

vyāpinī puruṣā 'nantyād bhogāya kurute yataḥ
sarvakāryāṇi sarvatra strotobhirviśvadhāmabhiḥ

taduktaṁ bṛhaspatipādaiḥ api sarvasiddhavācaḥ kṣīyeran dīrghakālam udgīrṇāḥ. māyāyāmānanatyānnocyate srotasāṁ saṁkhyā. iti eṣā ca kṣīradadhinyāyena na sarvātmanā pariṇāmameti kintu ghṛtakīṭanyāyenaikadeśeneti mantavyam.

(121B-122A)

sargasthitilayāstasyāḥ svātmasaṁsthāḥ prakīrtitāḥ
svātmasaṁsthaṁ vikārasya tattvādibhuvanā 'vadheḥ

evaṁ paramopādānatvānmāyāsthā eva jagataḥ sargādayaḥ bhuvanādeśca vikārasya tattvādisvarūpaṁ svātmasaṁstamiti tattvabhāvabhūtabhuvanātmakaṁ ca samastaṁ jagad vikārasthameva jñeyam. nanu śuddharūpamapi tattvādikaṁ tadupādānaṁ ca bindusaṁjñamāgameṣu śrūyate. satyam. tatprāptervidyeśvarādipadaprāptirūpatvenā'paramuktitvānnā' trā 'sya bhogasādhanatayopādānamityavirodhaḥ. atra ca.

(122B)

sargasthitī samākhyāte layaḥ sargaviparyayāt

pratitattvamutpattikramakathanena vyāpārapradarśanena ca sargasthitī prokte. layastu sargaprātilomyena svasvakāraneṣūpasaṁhāra ityarthaḥ. etcca.

(123A)

bhavasyānādimattvācca sargādiguṇanācyutam

anādirayaṁ saṁsāra ityarthaḥ. nanu bhogasādhanatvādātmanāṁ yukte sargasthitī. layastu kimarthamīśvareṇa kriyate. atra vadāmaḥ anvaratamanantapuruṣabhogajananopacitaśaktermāyāyāḥ-śukumāravanitāyā iva svāpena sāmarthyopodbalanārthamātmanāṁ viśramārthaṁ ca karmapākārthaṁ ca saṁhāra ityadoṣaḥ. taduktaṁ śrīmanmṛgendre. tacca sātmakamākramya viśramāyā' vatiṣṭhate. bhavināṁ bhavakhinnānāṁ sarvabhūtahito yataḥ. svāpe 'vyāste bodhayan bodhayogyān rodhyān rundhan pācyan karmikarma. māyāśaktīrvyaktiyogyāḥ prakurvan pācyan sarvaṁ yadyathā vastujātam iti. itthamātmanaḥ pratipāditaṁ sasādhanaṁ bhogamupasaṁhartuṁ tasyaiva malātmakam pāśamupakṣeptuṁ cāha.

(123B-124A)

puṁsāṁ māyāmayam bhogyaṁ māyotthaireva sādhanaiḥ
yato bhoktā viśuddhātmā cetanastanna cetanam

uktavat sukhādirūpaṁ buddhibodhātmakaṁ bhogyam māyākāryameva na tvātmani guṇatvena samavaiti. cetanatvāt. tatsamavāye puruṣasya pariṇāmādidoṣaprasaṅgācca. tasya ca cetanaḥ puruṣa eva bhoktetyuktam. sa ca vakṣyamāṇavadaviśuddhatvādāvṛtajñānakriyātvānmāyotthaiḥ kalādibhistattvairupabṛmhita eva tadbhoktuṁ śaknoti. kāryakāraṇaṁ vinā kiñcit jñātvāderapyadarśanāt. atha kuto' yamaviśuddhātmā 'ta āha.

(124B)

viṣayitvamalacchannasarvajñānakriyo yataḥ

yato 'yamātmā śivavat sarvajñānakriyāyukto 'pi kiñcidviṣaye vijñānàdau kalādikamapekṣate. yataśca muktasyā 'bhoktṛtvaṁ sarvaviṣayajñānādiyuktatvaṁ śrūyate tato 'yam viṣayitvākhyabhoktṛtvasya hetvād viṣayitvākhyena malenāvṛto 'vasīyate. yacchrūyate bhoktṛtvaṁ malataḥ proktam iti ata evā 'yamaviśuddhaḥ. taduktaṁ śrīmatsvāyambhuve. yadyaśuddhirna puṁso 'sti saktirbhogeṣu kiṁkṛte 'ti. ataśca.

(125A)

bījasthakarmarāgeṇa māyāmeṣo 'nudhāvati

karmaṇaḥ kṛṣyādivadātmasaṁskāratvā 'yogāt. bhavāsthāyāṁ buddhigatena pralaye naṣṭabuddherapi māyātmani jagadbīje pratisaṁcarārāt tatsthena paripākavaśād bhogajanakena karmātmanā rāgeṇa mārgeṇa māyāṁ bhogasādhanādirūpeṇa pariṇatāmeṣa pumānanusarati. atra paraḥ.

(125B-126A)

bhavāntarakṛtaṁ karma jātyādiphaladaṁ nṛṇāṁ
aśuddhiḥ kalpitā puṃsastasmin satyatiricyate

anāditvena bījāṅkuranyāyena kāryaśarīrabandhasyāvasthiterjātyāyurbhogapradāni karmāṇyeva svaphalabhogārthamātmanaḥ śarīrayogaṁ kurvantu. kiṁ malena bhavatā 'pi hi taṁ malaṁ kalpayitvā bhogavaicitryānyathānupapattyā karmā' pi kalpayate tataḥ kalpanāgauravaprasaṅgāt karmaiva kalpyatām. yadāhuḥ kalpyaṁ punarniruṇaddhi kalpanāmiti. atra parihāraḥ.

(126B-127A)

janmādijanikā śaktiḥ karmaṇo na malaṁ vinā
aṇurajñānarahitaḥ kvacijjāto na dṛśyate

ajñānahetunā malena rahitasya muktātmano janmādarśanāt karmānuṣṭhānādarśanācca malayuktasyaiva karmārjanaṁ tadbhogo vā upayujyate. yadyevaṁ malasyaiva janmādihetutvamastu kiṁ karmaṇeti codayati.

(127B-128A)

viṣayitvam hi tasyaikamastu kiṁ tena karmaṇā
yato janmādisaṁbandhamanusaṁprā-pnuyād dhruvam

pariharati.

(128B-129A)

santi kevalino jñānagrastāḥ karmavinākṛtaḥ
na ca janmādisaṃvandho dvayaṁ teneha kāraṇam

vijñānakevalināṁ malāvṛtānāmapi karmarahitānāṁ janmādyadarśanād dvayamapi māyāyoge heturityarthaḥ. nanu sṛṣṭeḥ prāg niṣkalatvāccetanatvāccātmanaḥ śivavadajñatvaṁ na yujyate iti parāśaṅkāṁ nirasyati.

(129B-130A)

prāksṛṣterniṣkalo janturdṛkkriyāguṇavān yataḥ
tataścājñānasaṁbandho nāyamityanṛtam vacaḥ

yadyevaṁ śivavadeva kalāsaṁbandho 'pyasya na yujyate tataśca kalāsambhandā 'nyathā 'nupapattyā tasya malo' bhyupagantavya. ityarthaḥ etadevāha.

(130B-131A)

dṛkkriye sarvaviṣaye sarvagatvādaṇormate
sarvajñaḥ sarvakṛt tasamāt sutṛptaḥ kāraṇaṁ vinā

na caitadevaṁ kiñcajjñatvādāvapi kalādyapekṣitvādityāha.

(131B)

kalādivyañjakābhā vānna vyakte tasya dṛkkriye

na caitadanāvaraṇasya yujyata ityāha.

(132A)

na hyanāvaraṇaṁ tejo bhānorvyañjakamīkṣate

ataśca.

(132B)

anādyanādisambandho malaḥ sādhāraṇo 'kṣayaḥ

anādiścāsāvātmanāmanādisaṁbandhaścānādyāvārakaḥ sarvapuruṣānāmeka eva. ata eva nityaśca malo' bhyupagantavyaḥ. yadyevaṁ malasya nityatvāt kadācidapyātmabhyo na nivṛttiḥ. nivṛttau va tasyaikatvādekapuruṣamokṣakāle sarvamokṣaprasaṅgo 'ta āha.

(133A)

pratipuṁniyataḥ svasvakālavyāvṛttaśaktikaḥ

malasya pratyātmaniyatānantaśaktiyuktatvādekasyāḥ śakteḥ pariṇāmavaśānnirodhe kṛte tasyaiva mokṣo nānyasya. yacchrūyate pratyātmasthasvakālāntopādhiśaktisamūhavat iti. nanu prākṛta eva viparyayarūpo mahāmohākhyo malo 'stu tasyāstata eva vyañjakāpekṣā karmānuṣṭhānaṁ copapadyate. ata āha.

(133B-134A)

mahāmohodbhavāt pūrvamaṇureṣa nirañjanaḥ
na śakyojjhayituṁ tenāsamvṛttaḥ sarvavat svayam

mahāmohasya kalādisambandhottarakālabhāvitvāt prathamataḥ sargārambhe bhavatpakṣe nirmalatvena śivavadanāvṛtaḥ pumāṃstena prākṛtamalenojjhayituṁ na śakyate. ato 'nādinā malenātmano 'nādisaṃbandho' bhyupagantavyaḥ. anyathā tu.

(134B-135A)

ādimān yadi sambandha iṣṭaḥ puṃmalayorbudhāh
tasyāpi kāraṇam vācyamiti nāsti vyavasthitiḥ

(135B-136A)

atha nirhetuko yogaḥ kalāyogo 'pyahetukaḥ
anirmokṣaśca jantūnāmīśābhāvaśca jāyate

nirhetukasya pāśasamsargasyābhyupagame śarīrādiyogasyā' pi nirhetukatvānmuktasyāpi punaḥ saṃsārayogādanirmokṣaḥ. sivasya 'pi pāśasaṃsargādanīśvaratvaṁ prasajyate. ato' nādireva malasambandhaḥ paśossaṃsāraheturabhyupeyaḥ. evaṁ malasyā 'sādhāraṇatve pratipuruṣamanekatve' bhyupagamyamāne jaḍatve satyanekatvād ghaṭadivadanityatva-prasaṅgaḥ. tataścānāditvābhāvātprāgukto 'nava sthānānirmokṣādidoṣaḥ syādityāha.

(135B-137A)

asāmānyo yadi bhavedacaitanye tvanekataḥ
utpādavān vināśī ca tataḥ pūrvoktadoṣabhāk

anāditvādeva cāsya nāntavatvaṁ tadyoge vā sarvānityatvaprasaṅga ityāha.

(137B-138A)

anādyanādisambandho yadi ceṣṭo vinaśvaraḥ
māyāśivātmavastūnāmajānāṁ nāśa iṣyatām

ittham prāk pratijñātaṁ malasyānāditvaṁ sādhāraṇatvam-akṣayatvaṁ ca prasādhyānantaśaktiyuktatvamapi sādhayati.

(138B)

pratipuṃniyatāścāsya śaktayo guṇarodhikāḥ

ātmaguṇasya jñānakriyātmano rodhikāḥ. etacca prāgeva darśitam. paridṛśyamānabhogavaicitryānyathā 'nupapattyā tāsāṁ malaśaktīnāṁ pariṇāmakāle vaicitryaṁ siddhamityāha.

(139A-140A)

na kālaniyatistāsāṁ vinivṛttyai nirodhataḥ
anyathā yugapanmuktiḥ sarveṣāṁ cidvatāṁ bhavet
na ca sā dṛśyate tasmājjñeyāstāḥ sūkṣmalakṣaṇāḥ

evam cānādyāvārakatvānmala evā 'tmanaḥ sahajaḥ pāśaḥ. māyādayastu tadbhāvabhāvino bhāvāḥ sarve māyātmakāḥ paśoḥ ityādiśrīmatsvāyambhuvādiśruterāgantukā eva jñeyāḥ. nanu śrīmanmataṅgādau tu moho madaśca rāgaśca viṣādaḥ śosa ityādinā mohādīnāmapi malahetutvaṁ sahajamalatvaṁ ca śrūyate. ata āha.

(140B-141A)

vṛttayo viṣayitvasya madādyāḥ pañca nocitāḥ
niṣkalātmani tasyaite no dṛṣṭā jātucid yataḥ

yato vijñānakalapralayākalayoḥ kalādisambandharahitatayā male satyapi vakṣyamāṇamadādayo na dṛśyante. kintu sakala eva. ato na malasyaite jñānakriyāvaraṇavad vṛttitveneṣṭāḥ. śrīmanmataṅgādau tu malasadbhāva eva māyopādānānāmanātmādāvātmābhimānādirūpānāmeṣām madādīnāmutpadyamānatvāt kalādiyoge 'pi nirmalānāṁ māyāgarbhādhikāryādīnāṁ tadadarśanācca tena malena sahakāriṇā jāyanta iti sahajamalahetutvāt sahajaśabdenocyante. na tu malopadānātayetyavirodhaḥ. nanu malopādānā apyete pralayakevalāvasthāyāmanabhivyaktāḥ paścāt kalādisambandhādabhivyajyanta ityasya pakṣasya ko doṣo 'ta āha.

(141B-142B)

bhogasādhanasambandhād vyajyanta iti nocitam tvayā tu
guṇavṛttibhyo ye proktā bhinnalakṣaṇāḥ bhavatā
guṇavṛttibhyo bhedenaiva madādayaḥ

proktā iti. na teṣām bhogasādhanasambandhāt paścādabhivyaktirutpadyate. etaduktaṁ bhavati. madādīnāṁ hi malopādānatve 'bhyupagamyamāne tasya sarvadaikarūpatvādabhivyaktyanabhivyaktabhedānutpattestatkāryabhūtajñānakriyāvaraṇavat saṃhārāvasthāyāmapyupalabhyeran. na copalabhyante. api tu bhogasādhanasaṃbandhottarakālamantaḥkaraṇasaṃsthā eva puṃsāmupalabhyante. ato malena sahakāriṇā māyodbhūtaguṇopādānā eva te' bhyupagantavya iti. athaiṣām guṇātmakatvameva darśayanti.

(143A143B)

madamohāvabhiṣvaṅgaḥ paritāpabhramau ca yau
tāmasau sāttvikaścaiva rājasau ca yathākramam

evaṁ cāntaḥkaraṇasaṃsthānāṁ guṇānāṁ vṛttayastvimāḥ na caitadvyatiriktāḥ kāścinmalasya vṛttayo madādisaṃjñāḥ kasyāñcidavathāyāmātmani dṛśyante. ato na santyeva tā ityāha.

(144A)

ābhyo bhinnā na mūlasya vṛttayo 'to na santi tāḥ

ataśca.

(144B-145A)

tyaktvā nirodhikāḥ śaktīrnānyo dharmo sya vidyate
karmāśayasametasya hetutvam ca bhaved bhave

kevalamalasya jñānakriyāvārakataṁ karmasaṃskārayuktasya saṃsārahetutvaṁ ca yuktisiddham. nānyat kāryāntaramityarthah. ittham malasvarūpamapi pradarśyopasaṃharati.

(145B)

paśurityaṁ samākhyāto yatsambandhādanuḥ paśuḥ

paśuśabdo malavācakatayā śrīmadrauravādau dṛśyate. tasya ca na tattvāntaratā. api tu paśutattva evāntarbhāvaḥ. tena vinā 'tmanāṁ paśutvā 'yogāt. tenānādyāvṛtatvācca kiñca vidhau sṛṣṭikāle śivasya sṛṣṭyādikaraṇapūrvamātmanāṁ bhogabhojanātmako māyāyāśca bhogasādhanakalādyutpādanatatpoṣaṇātmakaḥ paśvātmanāṁ ca bhogyabhogarūpo vyāpāro 'smin prakaraṇe proktaḥ. ete caiṣām vyāpārā ātmāvārakamalādeva hetubhūtād bhavanti. malasadbhāva eva 'sya sarvasya pravṛtteriti. api ca madādayaśca kleśāḥ puṃsāmatraiva pradarśitā ityupasaṃharan adhikārabhedāteṣām vṛttibhedānāha.

(146A-146B)

prasuptā tattvalīnānāṁ taṭaruddhāśca yoginām
vicitrodārarūpāśca kleśā viṣayasaṅginām

māyātattvalīnānāṁ pralayākalānāmete kleśāḥ guṇādīnāmapi tattvānām tattraivopasaṃhārāt prasuptā akiñcitkarā āsate. yogināṁ tvabhivyaktā api yogabalānmadhye niruddhavyāpārā bhavanti viṣayasaṅginām tu sakalānāṁ paśūnāmudbhūtavividhasvavyāpārā bhavanti. vicchinnodārarūpā iti paṭhe parasparamudbhvābhibhavābhyāṁ kadācidvicchinnarūpāḥ kadāciccodārarūpāśca bhavantītyarthaḥ. itthaṁ prakpratijñātayoḥ sasādhanayorbhogamokṣayoḥ. sasādhano bhogastāvadetābhiḥ pradarśita ityatraiva bhogaprakara-ṇopasaṁhāraḥ. mokṣastu sasādhanaḥ prakaraṇāntare pradarśayiyiṣyata iti. śubham.

śrīmatkheṭakanandanena guruṇā siddhāntasiddhiḥ sphuṭaṁ
saṁkṣepāditikārikābhirudito bhogaḥ samaṁ sādhanaiḥ.
vācastasya samīkṣya vītatapasā 'ghorādinā śambhunā
leśād deśikakuñjareṇa vivṛtistāsāmiyaṁ nirmitā.

samāpteyam bhogakārikā. ityaghoraśivācāryaviracitā bhogakārikāvṛttiḥ saṃpūrṇā.

BIBLIOGRAPHICAL REFERENCES (I)

Aṣṭaprakaraṇam. Ed. by Pt. Śrī Vrajavallabha Dvivedī. Yogatantra Granthamālā [Vol. 12]. Varanasi: Sampurnananda Sanskrit University, 1988.

Aṣṭaprakaraṇa. (Vol. I: *Tattvaprakāśikā* by Bhojadeva, comm. Aghora Śiva: *Tattvasaṅgraha* by Sadyojyoti, comm. Aghora Śiva: *Tattvatrayanirṇaya* by Sadyojyoti, comm. Aghora Śiva. Vol. II: *Ratnatraya* by Śrīkaṇṭha, comm. Aghora Śiva: *Bhogakārikā* by Sadyojyoti, comm. Aghora Śiva; *Nādakārikā* by Rāmakaṇṭha, comm. Aghora Śiva; *Mokṣakārikā* by Sadyojyoti, comm. Rāmakaṇṭha; *Paramokṣanirāsakārikā* by Sadyojyoti, comm. Rāmakaṇṭha). Ed. Kṛṣṇa Śāstrī. 2 Vols. Devakoṭṭai: Śaiva Siddhānta Paripālana, 1923 and 1925.

Bhāṣya of Praśastapāda together with Nyāyakandalī of Śrīdhara. Ed. Vindhyeśvariprasāda Dvivedin. The Vizianagram Sanskrit Series, ed. Arthur Venis. Benaras: E.J. Lazarus, 1895.

Bhattacharya, Gopinath. *Tarka Saṁgraha-Dīpikā on Tarka Saṁgraha.* Trans. Gopinath Bhattacharya. Calcutta: Progressive Publishers, 1975.

Brahma-Mīmāṃsā with Śrīkaṇṭha-Śivācārya's Commentary. Ed. L. Śrīnivāsāchārya. Government Oriental Library Series,

Bibliotheca Sanskrita No. 30. Mysore: Governmental Oriental Library, 1903.

Biardeau, Madeleine. "*Ahaṃkāra*: The Ego Principle in the Upaniṣads." *Contributions to Indian Sociology,* 8 (1965).

Brahmasūtraśāṃkarabhāṣyam. Ed. Narayan Ram Acharya. Bombay: Satyabhamabai Pandurang, 1948.

Brunner, Héléne. "Les catégories sociales Védiques dans le sivaïsme du Sud." *Année,* 252 (1975), 411-443.

Brunner, Héléne. "*Le Sādhaka,* Personnage Oublie du Śivaïsme du sud." *Année,* 263 (1975), 411-413.

Chakrabarti, Kisor Kumar. *The Logic of Gotama.* Society for Asian and Comparative Philosophy. Monograph No. 5. Honolulu: The University Press of Hawaii, 1977.

Chattopadhyaya, Latika. *Self in Sāṃkhya Philosophy*. Calcutta: Roy and Chowdhury, 1982.

Chenakaswami, Saraswati, *Concept of Mind in Indian Philosophy*. New York: Asia Publishing, 1960.

Çlokavārttika. Trans. Ganganatha Jha. Bibliotheca Indica, No. 1183. Calcutta: Asiatic Society, 1908.

Dasgupta, Surendranath. *A History of Indian Philosophy*. 5 Vols. Delhi: Motilal Banarsidass, 1975.

Devasenapathi, V.S. *Śaiva Siddhānta*. Madras University Philosophical Series No. 7. Madras: University of Madras, 1974.

Deussen, Paul, *The Philosophy of the Upaniṣads*. Trans. by A. S. Geden, New York: Dover Publications, 1966.

Dharmakīrti. Pramāṇavārttika. Ed. Swami Dwarikadas Sastri. 2 Vols. Varanasi: Bauddha-Bharati, 1968.

Dignāga, on perception. Trans. and annotation Masaaki Hattori. Harvard Oriental Series, ed. David H.H. Ingalls. Vol 47. Cambridge, Massachusetts: Harvard University Press, 1968.

Filliozat, P.S. "Le *Tattvaprakāśā* du roi Bhoja et les commentaires d'Aghoraśivācārya et de Śrīkumāra." *Journal Asiatique*, (11971), 247-296.

Filliozat, P.S. ed. and trans. The Tantra of Svayabhu Vidyāpāda with the Commentary of Sadyojyoti. Indira Gandhi National Centre for the Arts. New Delhi: Motilal Banarsidass Publishers, 1994.

Fort, Andrew O. "Dreaming in Advaita Vedānta." *PEW*, 35.4 (1985), 377-386.

Franco, Eli. "Studies in the *Tattvopaplavasiṃha*." Journal of Indian Philosophy, 11 (1983), 147-166.

Gerow, Edwin. "Indian Poetics" *A History of Indian Literature*. Ed. Jan Gonda. Vo. 5, Fasc. 3. Wiesbaden: Otto Harrassowitz, 1977.

Gonda, Jan. "Medieval Religious Literature in Sanskrit." *A History of Indian Literature*. Ed. Jan Gonda. Vol. 2, Fasc. 1. Wiesbaden: Otto Harrassowitz, 1977.

Gonda, Jan. *Viṣṇuism and Śaivism*. New Delhi: Munshiram Manoharlal Publishers, 1976.

Hopkins, E. *Epic Mythology*. Encyclopedia of Indo-Aryan Research, ed. Georg Buhler, III, I.Strassbourg, 1915.

Hulin, Michel "Sāṁkhya Literaute." *A History of Indian Literature*. Ed. Jan Gonda. Vol. 6, Fasc. 3. Wiesbaden: Otto Harrassowitz, 1978.

Jayanta Bhaṭṭa's Nyāya-Mañjarī. Trans. Janaki Vallabha Bhattacharya. Vol. 1. Delhi: Motilal Banarsidass, 1978.

Jha, Ganganatha. *Pūrva Mīmāṃsā in its Sources*. Library of Indian Philosophy and Religion. Ed. S. Radhakrishnan. Vol.1. Banaras: Banaras Hindu University, 1964.

Johnston, E. H. *Early Sāṃkhya*. London: R.A.S. Prize Publication Fund, 1937.

Keith, Arthur Berriedale. *Indian Logic and Atomism*. New York: Greenwood Press, 1968.

Kumar, Shiv. "Knowledge and its Genesis in Sāṃkhya-Yoga." *BORI*, 62 (1980), 16-32.

—"Sāṃkhya-Yoga Concept of Time." *BORI*, 64 (1983), 129-135.

Larson, Gerald James. *Classical Sāṃkhya*. Santa Barbara: Ross-Erikson, 1979.

—"The Notion of *satkārya* in Sāṃkhya: Toward a Philosophical Reconstruction." *PEW*, (1984), pp. 31-48.

Mataṅgapāremeśvarāgama (Vidyāpāda avec le commentaire de Bhaṭṭa Rāmakaṇṭha.) Ed. and Intro. N.R. Bhatt. Publications de L'institut Français d'Indologie. No. 56. Pondicherry: Institut Français d'Indologie, 1977.

Matilal, Bimal Krishna. *Logic, Language and Reality*. Delhi: Motilal Banarsidass, 1985.

—*Perception*. Oxford: Clarendon Press, 1986.

Mishra, Umesha. *Conception of Matter*. Allahabad: Umesha Mishra, 1936.

Mokṣakāragupta. *Tarkabhāṣā*. Trans. Y. Kajiyama. Kyoto: 1966.

Mṛgendrāgama: Sections de la Doctrine et du Yoga (avec la Vṛtti de Bhaṭṭanārāyaṇakaṇṭha et la Dīpikā d'Agoraśivācārya). Trans. intro and notes M. Hulin. Publications de l'Institut Français d'Indologie, No. 63. Pondicherry: Institut Français d'Indologie, 1980.

Mṛgendrāgama (vidyāpāda). Trans. Narayanaswami Aiyer. Aiyer. *Siddhānta Dīpikā*, IV, V, VI (1900-1904).

Nagatomi, M. "*Arthakriyā*." *Adyar Library Bulletin*, 31-32 (1967-1968), 243-260.

Nyāyamañjarī of Jayanta Bhaṭṭa. Ed. Sūrya Nārāyaṇa Śukla. Kashi Sanskrit Series No. 106. Benaras: Jaya Krishna Das Haridas Gupta. 1936.

Nyāya-sūtra with Vātsyāyana's Bhāṣya. Trans. Mrinalkanti Gangopadhyaya with intro. by Debiprasad Chattopadhyaya. Calcutta: Indian Studies, 1982.

PadārthadharmaSaṁgrahah with Śrīdhara's Nyāyakandalī. Ed. Vindhyesvariprasada Dvivedin. Vizianagram Sanskrit Series, No. 6. Benares: E. J. Lazarus and Co., 1895.

Padārthadharmasangraha of Praçastapāda with the Nyāyakandalī of Çrīdhara. Trans. Ganganatha Jha. Benaras: E.J. Lazarus and Co., 1916.

Pandey, Kanti Chandra. *Bhāskarī*, Vol 3: *An English Translation of the Īśvara Pratyabhijñā Vimarśinī, With an Outline of the History of Śaiva Philosophy*. The Princess of Wales Saraswati Bhavana Texts, No. 84. Lucknow: Superintendent, Printing and Stationary, 1954.

Podgorski, Frank. "Śaṃkara's Critique of Sāṃkhyan Causality in the *Brahmasūtrabhāṣya*." *PEW*, (1984), 49-57.

Parrot, Rodney. "The Experience Called 'Reason' in Classical Sāṃkhya." *JIP*, 13 (1985), 235-264.

Pātañjalasūtrāṇi with the Scholium of Vyāsa and the Commentary of Vācaspati. Ed., Dājāvām Shāstrī Bodas. Bombay Sanskrit Series, No. XLVI. Bombay: The Department of Public Instruction, 1892.

Pramāṇavārttika of Dharmakīrti. Ed. Swami Dwarikadas Sastri. *Bauddha Bharati* Series, Varanasi: Bauddha Bharati, 1968.

Pratyabhijñāhṛdayam. Trans. Jaideva Singh. Delhi: Motilal Banarsidass, 1980.

Radhakrishnan, S. *The Principal Upaniṣads*. Ed., intro. and trans. S. Radhakrishnan. London: George Allen and Unwin Ltd., 1963.

Randle, H. N. *Indian Logic in the Early Schools*. Oxford: The Clarendon Press, 1930.

Rauravāgamaḥ. Ed. N. R. Bhatt. Intro. Jean Filliozat. 2 Vol. Publications de L'institut Français d'Indologie. Pondicherry: Institut Français d'Indologie, I, 1961; II, 1968.

Sadānanda, *Vedāntasāra*. Trans. Swami Nikhilananda. Calcutta: Advaita Ashrama, 1974.

Sāṃkhya Sūtra Vṛtti. Ed.and trans. Richard Garbe. Calcutta: Bibliotheca Indica, 1888.

Sarva-darśana-Saṁgraha. Trans. E. B. Cowell and A. E. Gough. Chowkhamba Sanskrit Series, Vol. X. Varanasi: The Chowkhamba Sanskrit Series Office, 1961.

Sastri, K. Kuppuswami. *A Primer of Indian Logic*. Madras: P. Varadachary and Co., 1932.

Śaivaparibhāṣā of Śivāgrayogin. Trans. S.S. Suryanarayana. Ed. R. Balasubramanian and V.K.S.N. Raghavan. Madras University Philosophical Series, 35. Madras: University of Madras, 1982.

Sastri, Umesha. *Conception of Matter*. Allahabad: Umesha Mishra. 1936.

Śataratnasaṅgraha of Śrī Umāpati Śivācārya. Trans. P. Thirugnanasambandhan. Madras: University of Madras, 1973.

Śataratna Saṁgraha with the Śataratnollekha. Ed. Panchānan *Śāstrī*. Tantrik texts, Vol XXII. Calcutta: Bibhupada Ghosh, 1944.

Shabara-Bhāṣya. Trans. Ganganatha Jha. 3 Vols. Baroda: Oriental Institute, 1934.

Shastri, Dharmendra Nath. *The Philosophy of Nyāya-Vaiśeṣika and its Conflict with the Buddhist Dignāga School*. Delhi: Bharatiya Vidya Prakashan, 1964.

Sinha, J. *Indian Psychology of Perception*. London: Kegan, Paul Kegan, Paul Trench and Co., 1934.

Śivajñāna Siddhiyār of Aruḷnandi Śivācārya. Trans. J.M. Nallaswami Pillai. Madras: Meykandar Press, 1913.

Sivaraman, K. *Śaivism in Philosophical Perspective*. Delhi: Motilal Banarsidass, 1973.

—"The Word as a Category of Revelation." *Revelation in Indian Thought*. Ed. Harold Coward and Krishna Sivaraman. Emeryville, California: Dharma Publishing, 1977, pp. 45-64.

Ślokavārttika of Śrī Kumārila Bhaṭṭa. Ed. Swami Dvarikadasa Sastri. Varanasi: Tara Publications, 1978.

Somaśambhupaddhati. Ed. and intro. T.H. Brunner-Lachaux. 3 Vols. Publications de l'Institut Français d'Indologie, no. 25. Pondicherry: L'Institut Français d'Indologie, 1963, 1968 and 1977.

Tantrāloka of Abhinavagupta with the Commentary by Rājānaka Jayaratha. Madhusudhan Kaul. Kashmir Studies and Text Series, Vol. 23, 28, 30, 35, 36, 39, 41, 47, 52, 57, Srinagar, 1918, seq.

Sovani, V.V. *A Critical Study of the Sāṃkhya System*. Poona Oriental Series, No. 11. Poona: Orienta Book Agency, 1935.

Staal, Frits. "Ritual, Grammar, and the Origins of Science in India." *JIP*, 10 (1982), 1-24.

Stcherbatsky, T. *Buddhist Logic*. Lenningrad: 1930.

Tarka-Saṁgraha of Annambhaṭṭa. Ed. and notes Y.V. Athalye; Intro. and Trans. M.R. Bodas. Bombay Sanskrit Series, No. LV. Poona: R.N. Dandekar, 1963.

"*Tattva-Kaṭṭalei.*" Trans. Rev. Henry K. Hoisington. *JSOS,* IV (1854), 1-29.

Tattva-Kaumudī. Trans. Ganganatha Jha. Bombay: Theosophical Society Publication Fund, 1896.

"*Tattvaprakāśa* du Roi Bhoja et les Commentaires de Aghoraśivācārya et deŚrīkumāra." *Journal Asiatique,* (1971), 247-296.

Tattvaprakāśah by Bhojadeva with Śrīkumāra's Tātparyadīpikā and Aghoraśivācārya's Vṛttiḥ. Ed. Kamesvara Natha Mishra. Varanasi: Chaukhamba Orientalia, 1976.

Tattvasaṅgraha of Śāntarakṣita with the Commentary of Kamalaśīla Trans. Ganganatha Jha. Gaekwad's Oriental Series, No. LXXXIII. 2 Vol. Baroda: Oriental Institute, 1926.

Tucci, G. *Pre-Diṅnāga Buddhist Texts on Logic from Chinese Sources.* Gaekwad's Oriental Series, No. XLIX. Baroda: Oriental Institute, 1929.

Van Butenen, J.A.B. "Studies in Sāṃkhya." *JAOS,* I, LXXVI (1956), 155-157; II, LXXVII (1957) 15-25; III, LXXVII (1957), 88-107.

Vedāntasāra of Sadānanda. Trans. Swami Nikhilananda. Calcutta: Advaita Ashrama, 1949.

Vedānta Sūtras with the Commentary of *Śaṅkarācārya.* Trans. George Thibaut. Sacred Books of the East, Vol. XXXIV. 2 Vol. Oxford: Oxford University Press, 1904.

Warder, A.K. *The Science of Criticism in India.* Madras: The Adyar Library and Research Centre, 1978.

Woodroffe, Sir John. *Introduction to Tantra Śāstra.* Madras: Ganesh and Company, 1913.

Woods, James Haughton. *The Yoga-System of Patañjali.* Harvard Oriental Series, 17. Delhi: Motilal Banarsidass, 1977.

Yuktidīpikā. Ed. Ram Chandra Pandeya. Delhi: Motilal Banarsidass, 1967.

BIBLIOGRAPHICAL REFERENCES (II)

General Bibliography

Alper, Harvey P. "Śiva and the Ubiquity of Consciousness." *JIP,* 7 (1979), 345-407.

Aiyer, K.A.S. and K.C. Pandey. "Śaiva Theory of Relation." *Proceedings of the All-India Oriental Conference,* 9 (1940), 603-617.

Arapura, J. G. *Religion as Anxiety and Tranquility.* Religion and Reason, 5. The Hague: Mouton, 1972.

Arunachalam, M. *An Introduction to the History of Tamil Literature.* Tiruchitrambalam: Gandhi Vidyalayam, 1974.

Ayyar, C. V. Naryana. *Origin and Early History of Śaivism in South India.* Madras University Historical Series, No. 6. Ed. K. A. Nilakantha Sastri. Madras: University of Madras, 1974.

Bagchi, Amalendu. *Indian Definition of Mind.* Calcutta Sanskrit College Research Series No. XCVIII. Calcutta: Sanskrit College, 1975.

Bastow, David. "*An Attempt to Understand Sāṃkhya-Yoga.*" *JIP,* 5 (1978), 191-207.

Bhattacharyya, Gopikamohan. *Studies in Nyāya-Vaiśeṣika Theism.* Calcutta Sanskrit College Research Series, No. 14. Calcutta: Sanskrit College, 1961.

Bijalwan, C.D. *Indian Theories of Knowledge.* New Delhi: Heritage Publishers, 1977.

Brunner, Hélène. "Analyse du *Kiraṇāgāma.*" Année, 253 (1956), 309-328.

—"Analyse du *Suprabhedāgama.*" Année, 225 (1967), 31-60.

—"Importance de la literature agamique pour l'etudes des religions vivantes de l'Inde." *Indologica Taurinensia,* 3-4 (1975-1976), 107-124.

Chatterji, Jagadisha Chandra. *Kashmir Shaivism.* Srinagar: Research and Publication Department of the Government of Jamnu and Kashmir, 1962.

Chakravarty, Chintaharan. *The Tantras – Studies on their Religion and Literature.* Calcutta: Punthi Pustak, 1963.

Chatterji, Jagadisha Chandra. *The Hindu Realism.* Allahabad: The Indian Press, 1912.

Collected Lectures on Śaiva Siddhānta, 1946-1954. Ed. G. Subramania Pillai. Tiruppanandal Endowment Lectures. Annamalainagar: Annamalai University, 1965.

Das, Umesh Chandra. "Problems and justifications of the Theory of *Dṛṣṭisṛṣṭi.*" *JIP*, 5 (1977), 157-161.

Danielou, Alain. *Shiva and Dionysus.* Trans. K.F. Hurry. London: East-West Publications, 1984.

Desai, M.R. *The Yoga Sūtras of Patañjali.* Kolhapur: Prin. Desai Publication Trust, 1972.

Devasenapathi, V.A. *Śaiva Siddhanta as Expounded in the Śivajñāna Siddhiyār and its Six Commentaries.* Madras University Philosophical Series No. 7. Madras: University of Madras, 1974.

Dhavamony, Mariasusai. *Love of God According to Śaiva Siddhānta.*Oxford: Oxford University Press, 1971.

Doraiswami Pillai, Avvai, *A History of Tamil Literature.* Annamalai: Annamalai University, 1958.

Durairangaswami. *The Religion and Philosophy of Tevaram.* 2 Vols. Madras: University of Madras, 1959.

Dunuwilla, Rohan A. *Śaiva Siddhanta Theology: A Context for Hindu-Christian Dialogue.* Delhi: Motilal Banarsidass, 1985.

Farquhar, J.N. *Outline of the Religious Literature of India.* Oxford: Oxford University Press, 1920.

Frauwallner, Erich *Aus der Philosophie der Śivaitischen System.* Deutsche Akademie der Wissenschaften zu Berlin, Vortrage und Schriften, Heft 78. Berlin: Akadamie-Verlag, 1962.

Gangopadhyaya, Mrinalkanti. *Indian Atomism.* Bagchi Indological Series I. Calcutta: K.P. Bagchi and Co., 1980.

—*Indian Logic in its Sources.* New Delhi: Munshiram Manoharlal Publishers, 1984.

Gengnagel, Jörg. *Māyā, Puruṣa und Śiva.* Wiesbaden: Harrassowitz Verlag, 1996.

Gourdrian, Teun and Gupta Sanyukta. "Hindu Tantric and Śakta Literature." A History of Indian Literature. Ed. Jan Gonda. Vol. II, Fasc. 2. Wiesbaden: Otto Harrasowitz, 1981.

Hacker, Paul. "The Sāṅkhyization of the Emanation Doctrine Shown in a Critical Analysis of Texts." *Wiener Zeitschrift für die Kunde Sud- and Ostasiens* (*Archive für Indische Philosophie*), 5 (1961), 75-112.

Hacker, Paul. *Vivarta: Studien zur Geschichte der illusionistischen Kosmologie und Erkenntnis Theory der Inder.* Wiesbaden: Akademie der Wissenschaften und der Literature in Mainz, 1963.

Hara, Minoru. "Lillian Silburn, *La Bhakti.*" *Indo-Iranian Journal* 9 (1966), 211-218.

Hart, George Luzerne. "The Relation Between Tamil and Classical Sanskrit Literature." *A History of Indian Literature.* Ed. Jan Gonda. Vol. X, Fasc. 2. Wiesbaden: Otto Harrasowitz, 1976.

Hindu Theology: A Reader. Ed. Jose Pereira. New York: Image Books, 1976.

Jash, Pranabananda. *History of Śaivism.* Calcutta: Roy and Chaudhury, 1974.

Jesudasan, C. *A History of Tamil Literature.* Calcutta: YMCA Publishing House, 1961.

Kalupahana, David J. *Causality: The Central Philosophy of Buddhism.* Honolulu: The University Press of Hawaii, 1975.

Kaw, R.K. *The Doctrine of Recognition (Pratyabhijñā Philosophy)* Vishveshvaranand Indological Series Vol. 40. Hoshiarpur: Vishveshvaranand Institute, 1967.

Kent, Stephen A. "Early Sāṃkhya in the *Buddhacarita.*" *PEW,* 32.3 (1980), 259-278.

Klostermaier, Klaus. "Time in Patañjali's *Yogasūtra.*" *PEW,* 34-2 (1984), 205-210.

Kulathungam, L.C.D. "Buddhist Elements in the Logic of Śaiva Siddhānta." Śaiva Siddhānta, 29 (1970), 171-183.

Kumar, Shiv. "Jayantabhaṭṭa's Critique of the Sāṃkhya Concept of Sequential Stages of Evolution." *BOKI,* LX (1979) 158-165.

Larson, Gerald James. "An Eccentric Ghost in the Machine: Formal and Quantitative Aspects of the Sāṃkhya-Yoga Dualism." *PEW,* 33.3 (1983), 219-233.

Larson, Gerald James. "The Format of Technical Philosophical Writing in Ancient India: Inadequacies of Conventional Translations." *PEW,* 30.3 (1982), 375-380.

Malladevru, H.P. *Essentials of Vīraśaivism.* Bombay: Bharatiya Vidya Bhavan, 1973.

Mānikka-Vācagar. *The Tiruvācagam.* Trans. G.U. Pope. Oxford: University of Oxford, 1900.

Masson, J.Ḷ. "Sex and Yoga: Psychoanalysis and the Indian Religious Experience." *JIP*, 2 (1974), 307-320.

Mathews, Gordon. *Śiva-ñāna-bōdham.* Trans. G. Mathews. Oxford: Oxford University Press, 1948.

Motilal, Bimal Krishna. Nyāya-Vaiśeṣika. "*A History of Indian Literature*" Ed. Jan Gonda. Vol. VI, Fasc. 2. Wiesbaden: Otto Harrasowitz, 1977.

Mishra, Kamalakar. *Significance of the Tantric Tradition.* Varanasi: Arddhanarisvara Publications, 1981.

Mohanty, J.N. "Consciousness and Knowledge in Indian Philosophy." *PEW*, 29.1 (1971), 3-10.

Mudaliyar, S. Arumuga. "Śaiva Siddhānta Works (*Sattiram* and *Tottiram*) in Tamil." *Bharatiya Vidya,* 23 (1963), 76-79.

Murti, T.R.V. *The Central Philosophy of Buddhism.* London: Allen and Unwin, 1970.

Nagaswamy, R. *Tantric Cults of South India.* Delhi: Agaṃ Prasad Prakashan, 1982.

Nyāyadarśanam. Ed. Taranatha Nyaya-Tarkatirtha. Calcutta: Metropolitan Printing and Publishing House, 1936.

O'Flaherty, Wendy Doniger. *Śiva, The Erotic Ascetic.* New York: Oxford University Press, 1973.

Pandey, Kanti Chandra. *Abhinavagupta: An Historical and Philosophical Study.* 2nd ed. Chowkhamba Sanskrit Series, Vol. I. Varanasi: Chowkhamba Sanskrit Series Office, 1963.

Paranjoti, V. "The Siddhāntin's Criticism of *Māyāvāda.*" Philosophical Quarterly, 10 (1934-1935), 171-188.

Parrot, Rodney J. "The Problem of the Sāṃkhya Tattvas as Both Cosmic and Psychological Phenomenon." *JIP,* 14 (1986), 55-77.

Pāśupata Sūtras with Panchārthabhāṣya of Kauṇḍinya. Ed. R. Ananthakrishna Sastri. University of Travancore Series No. I. Trivandrum: University of Travancore, 1940.

Phillips, Steven H. "The Conflict of Voluntarism and Dualism in the *Yogasūtra.*" *JIP,* 13 (1985), 399-414.

Piet, John H. *A Logical Presentation of the Śaiva Siddhānta Philosophy.* Indian Research Series Vol. VIII. Madras: The Christian Literature Society for India, 1952.

Pillai, J.M. Nallaswami. *Śivajñāna Botham of Meikaṇḍa Deva.* Madras: Sri La Sri Somasundara Nayagar, 1895.

Ponniah, V. *Theory of Knowledge of Śaiva Siddhānta.* Annamalai University Philosophy Series IV. Annamalainagar: Annamalai University, 1962.

Prasad, Hari Shankar. "Time and Change in Sāṃkhya-Yoga." *JIP,* 12 (1984), 35-49.

Reller, Carl A. "Śaiva Siddhānta (Philosophic Religieuse de I'inde du Sud)." *Asiatische Studien,* 32.1(1978), 97-122.

Rosu, Arion. "Yoga et Alchemie." *Zeitschrift der Deutschen Morgenlandischen Gesellshaft,* 32.2 (1982), 364-379.

Saksena, S.K. *Nature of Consciousness in Hindu Philosophy* Delhi: Motilal Banarsidass, 1971.

Sāṃkhya-sūtras of Pañcaśikha and the Sāṃkhyatattvāloka. Trans. Swami Hariharananda Aranya and Intro. Jajneswar Ghosh. Delhi: Motilal Banarsidass, 1977.

Sastri, S.S. Suryanarayana. *The Śivādvaita of Śrīkaṇṭha.* Madras: University of Madras, 1972.

Scherrer-Schaus, Christina. "Le Terme *Yukti*: Premiére Étude." *Asiatische Studien Etudes Asiatiques,* 35.2 (1981), 189-199.

Schomerus, H.W. *Der Çaiva Siddhānta.* Leipzig: J.C. Hinrichs'sche Buchhandlung, 1912.

Schrader, F. Otto. *Introduction to the Pañcarātra and the Ahirbudhnya Saṃhitā.* Madras: Adyar Library, 1916.ss

Secret Doctrine of Recognition (Pratyabhijñāhṛdayam). Ed. by the staff of the Adyar Library and trans. Kurt F. Leidecker. Madras: Adyar Library, 1983.

Sen, Debabrata. *The Concept of Knowledge: Indian Theories.* Calcutta: K.P. Bagchi and Co., 1984.

Serpent Power. Trans. Sir John Woodroffe. Madras: Ganesh and Co., 1978.

Sharma, Arvind. "A Note on the Doctrine of 'Grace' in the Upaniṣads." *The Indian Journal of Theology,* 27.1 (1978), 28-30.

Sharma, Ram Murti. *"Concept of Puruṣa in Indian Philosophy."* Baroda Oriental Institute Journal, 30 (1980-1981), 165-171.

Shastri, S.S. *The Śivādvaita of Śrīkaṇṭha.* Madras: University of Madras, 1930.

Śivaraman, K. "*The Role of the Śaivāgama* in the Emergence of Śaivasiddhānta: A Philosophical Interpretation." "*Traditions in Contact and Change.*" Ed. Peter Slater and Donald Wiebe with Maurice Boutin and Harold Coward. Kitchener Waterloo: Wilfred Laurier Press, 1983, pp. 53-64 and 674-679.

Sinha, Debabrata. "Human Embodiment: The Theme and the Encounter in Vedāntic Phenomenology." *PEW*, 34.3 (1985) 230-247.

Śivādvaita-Nirṇaya of Appaya Dīkṣita. Madras University Philosophical Series, No. 22. Madras: University of Madras, 1974.

*Sivagñāna Botham of Meikaṇḍa Deva.*Trans. J.M. Nallaswami Pillai. Madras: Sri La Sri Somasundara Nayager, 1895.

Śiva Sahasranāma Stotra. Text and trans. R. Anantakrishna Sastri. Madras: V. Ramaswamy Sastrulu and Sons, 1955.

Śiva Sūtras. Trans. Jaideva Singh. Delhi: Motilal Banarsidass, 1979.

Soloman, Esther A. *The Commentaries of the Sāṃkhya Kārikā.* Ahmedabad: Gujarat University, 1974.

Spanda-Kārikās. Trans. Jaideva Singh. Delhi: Motilal Banarsidass, 1980.

Śrīkaṇṭha-Bhāṣya. Trans. Roma Chaudhuri. Pracyavani Research Series, Vol. XI, 2 Vol. Calcutta: Pracyavani, 1959.

Srinivasan, Doris M. "Vedic Rudra-Śiva." *JAOS*, 103.3 (1982), 543-556.

Steiner, Margarethe. "*Der Ahaṃkāra in den alteren Upaniṣden.*" Festgabe von Richard Garbe. *Aus Indian Kultur.* Veroffentlichungen des Indogermanischen Seminars der Universitat Erlangen. Band III. Erlangen: Palm and Enke, 1927.

Subrahmanyam, K. "The Metaphysics of the Śaiva Siddhānta System." *Proceedings of the All-India Oriental Conference*, 3 (1924), 569-582.

Sundaramoorthy, G. "Development of Epistemology in the Sanskrit Works of Śaiva Siddhānta." *Indian Philosophical Annual*, Vol. IV. Madras: University of Madras, 1981.

Timmerman, Heinz. "Vor-Sāṃkhyistisches und Proto-Sāṃkhyishsches in alten Upaniṣaden." *Asiatische Studien Études Asiatiques*, 35.2 (1981), 201-219.

Tirukkural. Trans. G.U. Pope, W.H. Drew, John Lazarus and F.W. Ellis. Madras: The South Indian Śaiva Siddhānta Works Publishing House, 1962.

Tiruvaçagam. Trans. Rev. G.M. Pope. Oxford: Oxford University Press, 1900.

Vijñānabhairava or Divine Consciousness. Trans. Jaideva Singh. Delhi: Motilal Banarsidass, 1979.

Viśvanāthapañcānanakṛtasiddhāntamuktāvalisahitabhāṣāparicchedaḥ. Ed. and trans. E. Roer. Bibliotheca Indica, ed. E. Roer. Vol. IX, Nos. 32 and 35. Calcutta: Asiatic Society of Bengal, 1850.

Watson, Ian K. "*Buddhi, Manas, Deha and Mokṣa.*" Indian Philosophical Quarterly, I (1976), 151-164.

INDEX